3/28/2003

Happy Birthday

2

The New Jersey Churchscape

Frank L. Greenagel

THE NEW JERSEY CHURCHSCAPE

Encountering Eighteenth- and Nineteenth-Century Churches

Rutgers University Press

NEW BRUNSWICK, NEW JERSEY

Library of Congress Cataloging-in-Publication Data

Greenagel, Frank L., 1939–

The New Jersey churchscape : encountering eighteenth- and nineteenth-century churches
/ Frank L. Greenagel.

p. cm.

Includes bibliographical references and index.

ISBN 0-8135-2990-5 (alk. paper)

1. Church buildings—New Jersey. 2. Church architecture—New Jersey—18th century.

3. Church architecture—New Jersey—19th century. I. Title.

NA5230.N5 G74 2002

726.5'09749—dc21   2001019804

British Cataloging-in-Publication data for this book is available from the British Library.

BOOK DESIGN AND TYPOGRAPHY BY JENNY DOSSIN

Manufactured in the United States of America

FOR

Bob and Ray and Suzanne

CONTENTS

PREFACE

IN THE LATTER PART of the nineteenth century the city hall or courthouse, the railroad station, and the dominant church provided important symbols for a town. The architect was expected to design a building that went beyond the merely functional to embody and affirm the significance of its sponsor. The number of churches that have survived for more than a century is one measure of their success, but the churches, like the railroad stations, have lost much of their symbolism, as the shopping mall and the stadium have become more potent tropes of our current aspirations. Nevertheless, the old churches remain of interest, visually, architecturally, and culturally, because they can help us understand where we have come from. My topic is the Jersey churchscape, not simply the architecture or the history of the early churches. My intention is not only to create a photographic inventory of the old churches in the state, but to arrange the images and place them in a context so that we may see them anew, for the first time.

I use the term *churchscape* to encompass not only the scale, design, materials, and setting, but the denomination of the original congregation and the architectural, cultural, and religious traditions associated with the church or region. Over the five years that I have been photographing the churches of New Jersey, some patterns have formed in my mind, and by arranging the images chronologically within three major regions of the state I hope to make those patterns more perceptible to the person not schooled in architectural history, as I am not. I am neither a historian nor an architect nor a believer, although I am well read in all three areas.

I estimate there are about eleven hundred eighteenth- and nineteenth-century church buildings that remain, a significant portion of them still in use as churches, although many now serve as private residences, social service offices, town halls, and museums. Many are exceptionally well documented, whereas others required extensive digging simply to identify the original denomination and the date of construction. In my home county, of the ninety-nine church buildings that remain, twenty-three no longer hold religious services; several are residences, one is a B&B, and two house volunteer fire companies. Three congregations have given up the ghost as this work was being prepared, merged with other congregations, and put their buildings up for sale. Not all are recognized as former churches, even by the inhabitants or by local historical societies.

I have photographed more than five hundred old churches, including 90 percent of those listed on the National Register of Historic Places. Only 225 appear in these pages, so a word about the selection criteria is appropriate. Almost all eighteenth-century churches in the regions I photographed are included, even where it may appear repetitive, as is the case with the many Quaker meetinghouses. Any building that has survived this long is worthy of the respect that can be shown by inclusion in a book on old churches. Where I could determine the earliest church of a particular denomination in a region, I have included it. Churches with an important history—not necessarily that George Washington held a court martial there, but that were influential in the development of the area or that illustrate a significant architectural style—are included. About two-thirds of the surviving churches were built since the Civil War, but less than half the images here are from that period. I have no aversion to the architecture of that era, but felt it important to include more of the earliest churches.

Interesting examples of architectural styles, including simple vernacular buildings, survived the filtering process. A building whose date of erection or original denomination could not be identified was not included, except in a couple of cases, although I am confident that, given sufficient time, I might have found someone who could have provided those essential details. I acknowledge a prejudice against aluminum siding, so where I had an alternative, I selected a church with original clapboards and cornices intact.

I made an effort to seek out and include churches of smaller religious sects, such as the Moravians, the Church of the Brethren, and the Seventh Day Baptists, because the diversity of religions in the state is an important theme that needs to be illustrated as well as spoken about. There are only six or seven nineteenth-century Jewish synagogues that remain; four of them are included here. I was concerned that there not be a disproportionate number of Presbyterian and Episcopal churches represented; many of them are especially fine buildings, but I felt it important also to attempt to represent the denominations in roughly the proportion they maintained at the end of the nineteenth century. That was not strictly possible inasmuch as the earliest surviving churches are Quaker, Episcopal, Presbyterian, and Baptist, but by the end of the nineteenth century, there were probably more Methodist churches in the state than those of any other denomination, and Catholic Church membership had far outstripped any single Protestant sect. So I am content with an adequate sample, if not a proportionate one.

There are a number of well-designed churches that did not make the cut; as will be seen, many churches were apparently built to the same plan, so I saw little need to include more than a few representative examples. Thus, the Simpson Methodist Church in Perth Amboy follows a style that is common to churches in more than fifteen west-central communities, all built about the same period, but of wood. Only the Liberty Corner and Pottersville churches are included here, but their form will be instantly recognizable by residents of High Bridge, Annandale, Clinton, White House, and Milford and a dozen other congregations.

Fixing the erection date of many churches was more difficult than I had imagined; two or three sources often gave different dates, some decades apart, although I rarely had even two sources for most churches. I have relied heavily on Ellis Derry's two books on old and historic churches and on the county history compendiums published in the early 1880s, fully cognizant that these older publications were, in many cases, written by the church's minister or a member of the congregation, neither of whom were necessarily particularly concerned with accuracy. Many of the churches have undergone several stages of construction, remodeling, and expansion. In a few cases, there is solid documentation for an erection date different from what is carved on the cornerstone, and in more than a handful of cases, the church was built before the congregation was officially organized, both of which can cause some confusion. Two relatively recent books, each written by an acknowledged authority, have placed the construction of the Presbyterian church in Cranbury in 1788 and 1859, respectively; for stylistic reasons, I have opted for 1839. I have used the date that seems most reliable and consistent with the architectural style and construction of the church; where there is some doubt, I have noted that.

In arranging the churches in chronological order, according to the date of construction, I expect partisans of some churches to argue for an earlier date than I have assigned. Everyone likes to claim as much antiquity as possible for his home, church, or organization. Many of the dates are well established, but there are a few like St. John's of Newark, whose date of erection is variably offered as 1826 or 1828. A careful reading of the sources available leads me to prefer 1858, when the church in its present form is first recognizable. I accept that there was a church on the site as early as 1828, but it does not appear to me that the church we see today is the church that a parishioner in 1830 would recognize.

Similarly, published sources seem to agree that St. Michael's Church in Trenton was built in 1753. I think that date is highly improbable, given the available records. The existence of an early foundation, or even an internal braced frame dating to an earlier building, is not sufficient for classifying the current building as belonging to a more ancient period. I have tried to place the building at its earliest supportable date, and noted any significant rebuildings, alterations, and renovations. I am reasonably confident that there are no gross errors in chronology that would have a material impact on any of the generalizations in this work.

Generalizing about anything concerning New Jersey is risky because exceptions abound. Speak of the architecture, construction, or even the early denominations found in a county, and within that region can often be found multiple examples that test the theory. Nevertheless, I have not been reluctant to generalize when I felt there was a pattern or relationship that might enrich our understanding of the churchscape. One of the few absolutes is that there are no Congregational churches in Hunterdon County and there have never been any, a fact of potential significance when one considers that only forty-five miles away, Newark was founded by Puritans moving down from Connecticut with the intent of setting up a religious colony. Somerset County has but two Congregational churches, which date to the nineteenth century, and even Essex and Union Counties, the locus of the early Puritan settlements, have only a handful. What struck me initially as simply a curious fact may help to explain why the religious architecture of New Jersey looks different from that of Congregational-dominated Connecticut and New England.

Even with the aid of old photographs it is often hard to visualize how some of the churches dominated their surroundings when today, tall steeples are dwarfed by a midsized office building, and substantial brick meeting-houses, once stark and massive, now nestle snugly beneath huge sycamores in a row of shops on Main or Broad Street. What once seemed isolated now lies around the corner from a major shopping center or residential concentration. I have not tried to recapture the past by separating the church from its urban setting or eliminating the cars, street signs, and power lines strung in front of almost every facade. In a few cases, I have emphasized those elements because what they detracted from the church itself they added to the photographic composition.

I have not encumbered the text with notes about film, lenses, filters, and f-stops, but note here that most were shot on TMax 100 film with a 4x5 view camera, generally with a long exposure using a yellow or green filter. That has produced some black skies in a few cases, but no attempt was made to manipulate the images in the darkroom or on the computer beyond a little burning or dodging. No automobiles, telephone poles, power lines, or other artifacts of modern life have been removed.

Prior to the preparation of this book I pored over photographic books on the wooden churches of Cape Breton Island, the adobe churches of New Mexico, and the small parish churches of England, as well as a number of volumes on the grand abbeys and cathedrals of northern Europe and a beautiful volume on the prairie schoolhouses of the Midwest. I have studied photographs of churches by Paul Strand, Walker Evans, Wright Morris, George Tice, and Bruce Barnbaum in particular; they transcend their subject matter, and I sought a perspective or principle in them that might aid me. There are only so many ways one can approach a white rectangular building without being horribly repetitive. The important things are (1) where you set your tripod, (2) what the light is like, and (3) what the sky is like. The rest is incidental.

I suspect this work is not yet done. I have seen only half the old churches in the state, or slightly more if you count those clothed in aluminum siding that I decided not to photograph. I believe there are more than a hundred churches built before 1860 that still exist but have been lost track of and now serve as residences or shops. I would like to follow up clues about churches that have been dismantled and carted off, or simply sold, often to a black congregation, and then disappeared from the historical record. And I expect to continue to explore the state with my camera. I am not committing myself to photographing all of the old churches, but I have not ruled it out. Readers who desire information about the several hundred old churches I have photographed and researched that are not included here are directed to a website I created and maintain; as of this writing, the URL is: www.njchurchscape.com.

A photographer works alone, especially in the darkroom, but a historian is indebted to others, and not just intellectually. The staff of the library at Raritan Valley Community College were especially helpful in locating and obtaining volumes for my research, as were librarians, whose names I did not get, at many municipal libraries. Charles Cummings of the Newark Public Library tracked down files, photographs, clippings, and people that I would have overlooked. My good friend John Churchill flew me over a number of churches, always above FAA minimums, but sufficiently low to enable some bird's-eye views from a Piper Cub that is even older than I am. Janet Sliker of the Lebanon Township Historical Commission, Peter Campbell of the Second Presbyterian Church in Elizabeth, and Kathy Gissner of the First Baptist Church in Woodstown provided me with fascinating tours and historical materials that saved me hours of research and enriched my understanding immensely. Bill Woodall located sources online and offered technical assistance in scanning and editing the digitized images. Mark Goodman provided me with information about the remaining synagogues of New Jersey, most of which I would never have found on my own. The largest debt is due Suzanne Lagay, who accommodated lengthy periods of reclusiveness and a fixation on colonial history and church architecture to the virtual exclusion of everything that sustains a relationship.

FRANK L. GREENAGEL

Holland Township, November 2000

The New Jersey Churchscape

THE CHURCHSCAPE

Diversity, Location, Construction, and Design

O NE OF THE LEADING architectural writers of the nineteenth century concluded in 1851 that American churches were the "ugliest in Christendom." A. J. Downing had some praise for church architecture in New York and Brooklyn, but he opined that "rural churches were sadly behind in taste and meritorious design; [they are] ill-proportioned and unmeaning, or crowned with steeples and towers, exhibiting the oddest possible combinations of architectural orders."[1] Downing advocated Gothic architecture as the most appropriate style for religious buildings, and the next

MOUNT LEBANON METHODIST EPISCOPAL CHURCH

half century was to see the ascendency of those views. Of the roughly eleven hundred churches in New Jersey that survive from the eighteenth and nineteenth centuries, more than two-thirds are Gothic in style. But we shall see that the term Gothic has been stretched to encompass an extremely wide variety of styles, so wide that one "Gothic" church may share no common elements with another "Gothic" church.

To look at religious architecture alone, however, is to misunderstand much of the meaning of church-building in previous centuries. I propose to examine the Jersey churchscape, which encompasses much more than the architectural style of the building, although that is what the average passerby notices, if he or she notices anything at all other than a quaint "Victorian" church. If we would understand the many ways the churchscape can inform our appreciation of the community, its history, and something of the cultural history of the people and the denomination who built it, we must expand the definition of *churchscape* to include the location and immediate setting, the scale or mass of the building, the churchyard, if there is one, the materials, and, of course, the architectural style and details. A fuller description of the churchscape then would include the date the building was erected, and when it was enlarged or modified. Certainly the year the congregation was organized is likely to help our understanding. We need to include the denomination and the nationality, or culture, of its builders, which is to say the first congregation. And today, it would include the later occupants and uses of that building, which reflect the changes in the neighborhood that have taken place since its erection. I have come to understand that a description of the Jersey churchscape is more than a photographic inventory.

My original intention was simply to photograph the old churches, but I got caught up in an attempt to find out when they were built and by whom, why they were sited where they are, and why they look the way they do. The explanation has less to do with architectural history and more with culture, immi-

LAMINGTON PRESBYTERIAN CHURCH

gration patterns, American history, and social aspirations. In those respects, the Jersey churchscape is not only different from the New England churchscape and the Virginia churchscape, but there are several churchscapes in the state, each visibly and culturally different. They primarily reflect the different settlement patterns, at least until the Civil War, when national styles began to overwhelm regional differences.

Think of the "typical" New England village, if you will. My mind's eye conjures up a white, frame clapboard building with a tall steeple, located on the village square or, if the place is really small, in the

GLEN GARDNER METHODIST
EPISCOPAL CHURCH

center of the one road through town. Apart from the steeple, it is recognizably a church, with a formal entrance and adjacent churchyard with old gravestones. If we move in a little closer and perhaps make some inquiries, we find it serves, or served, as the town meeting hall, for the Puritans who built it in the late eighteenth or early nineteenth century made no distinction between public and sacred issues. It is a Congregational church (the successor to the Puritans), the grandest building in town, and likely the only church in the immediate area. Here is a description of a half dozen churches written seventy years ago about an area along the Massachusetts–New Hampshire border.

> A cluster of country meetinghouses [dating to about 1810–1825] . . . situated in the southwest corner of New Hampshire and across the line in Massachusetts. . . . They are all set on high ground, fronting the village greens, with their backs to open meadow or woodland and, in two cases, a country graveyard. They can be seen from afar off and dominate, by bulk and height, each composition of town and landscape. . . . At the rear they are square without projections. Each has a bell and an open belfry. Each is surmounted by a tower and an enormous weathervane. The more sophisticated carry the town clock.[2]

A resident of Virginia would not recognize that description as accurate in the least. The "typical" old church in rural Virginia might remind many of us of a visit to Colonial Williamsburg and the church there, a red brick building set among the trees on a spacious plot. But just as often, that church would be located at a crossroads or near a river, rather than in the center of a village. The windows look different, generally because the tops are round, and there is a transept or crossing, giving the church a cruciform plan. There is a steeple or at least a belfry, but probably neither as tall nor as ornate as in New England. There is no town clock in the steeple. There is a churchyard, but the better-off families preferred private burial plots on their own estates. And the church is undoubtedly Anglican.

Few residents of New Jersey would find either description very apt, although there are churches that fit each one. A more likely sketch of the Jersey churchscape of the same period would include these elements:

The village church is as likely to be found on a remote plot, set among

MOUNT AIRY PRESBYTERIAN CHURCH, NEAR LAMBERTVILLE

woodlands and cornfields, as along a major road or in town. It might be made of wood, stone, or brick, depending on where in the state you are. It belongs to a Quaker, Presbyterian, Methodist, Baptist, or Reformed congregation, also depending on where you are, but probably not Anglican and almost certainly not Congregational. The building is not immediately recognizable as a church—it could be a country schoolhouse or the town hall; the belfry appears rather secular, and there is no special window treatment. If there is a tower, there is no clock in it, in any case. There is an adjacent graveyard with a low stone wall around it, which is the one sure sign that it is, indeed, a church.

ORIGINAL SACRED HEART ROMAN CATHOLIC CHURCH, MOUNT HOLLY

Residents of Essex and Hudson Counties might have trouble recognizing that description as appropriate for their area today, but their grandparents would not, nor would the residents of any other county in the state. It is not simply regional traditions that account for these differences, but the cultures and denominations that built the churches. Before we look at each of the regions in the state, let us consider the broad aspects of location, construction, and architectural styles.

Religious Diversity and Land Speculation

THERE ARE TWO fundamental reasons why the Jersey churchscape developed differently from that of other colonies: religious diversity and the settlement patterns that arose from the speculative activities of the colony's proprietors and early landholders.

The religious diversity of the state was set at an early stage (1665), when the original proprietors, Lord Berkeley and Sir George Carteret, eager to make money from their holdings by attracting settlers, drew up a series of Concessions and Agreements designed to make settlement inviting. These included a declaration of religious practice:

No person qualified as aforesaid [freeman] within the said province at any time shall be in any ways molested, punished, disquieted or called in question, for any difference in opinion or practice in matters of religious concernments, who do not actually disturb the peace of the said province; but that all and every such person and persons, may, from time to time, and at all times, freely and fully have and enjoy his and their judgments and consciences, in matters of religion, throughout the said province, they behaving themselves peaceably and quietly, and not using this liberty to licentiousness, nor to the civil injury or outward disturbance of others.[3]

Although that declaration did not immediately attract large numbers of immigrants, it did set a precedent for religious toleration in New Jersey that was largely observed from that time forward (except for the widespread discrimination against Catholics that persisted well into the twentieth century). In contrast is the Dutch West India Company's charter of Freedoms and Exemptions for their New Netherland colony (much of New Jersey was nominally under control of the Dutch proprietors) a generation earlier:

No other religion shall be publicly admitted in New Netherland except the Reformed, as it is at present preached and practiced by public authority in the United Netherlands.[4]

In a similar vein is a clause in the articles of incorporation of a proposed Dutch colony near the mouth of the Delaware River, Zwaanendael:

All eccentric persons such as obstinate papists which are strongly attached to the Roman chair, parasitic Jews, Anglican headstrong Quakers and Puritans, and rash and stupid believers in the millennium, besides all present-day pretenders to revelation, etc., will have to be carefully averted from this Christian civilian society.[5]

To make colonization pay, the Dutch West India Company belatedly realized they had to liberalize religious restrictions if they wanted to attract Lutherans, Jews (who held 10 percent of their stock), and Quakers, all of whom were important to the trade and commercial activities of New Amsterdam. The Dutch proprietors never resolved the tension between the

Dutch Reformed Church's restrictive policy and the tolerance demanded by settlers of other persuasions;[6] in 1664 the Dutch colony was overwhelmed by a small English force, and that opened the way for the ethnic and religious diversity that was to characterize New Jersey's earliest settlements.

The particular legacy of those Concessions and Agreements issued the year following the English takeover is the significant diversity of nationalities and religious sects found in the country even fifty years after its initial settlement. Prior to 1710 English policy had been to discourage non-English immigration. Under the influence of mercantilist theory, which held that the economic strength of a nation lies partly in the size of its population, that policy was reversed sometime after 1710, when English governments tolerated and in some cases even subsidized European immigration, though English emigration to North America was discouraged.

Berkeley soon gave up on his prospects for quick financial gain and sold his share to two Quakers, who quickly transferred title to several other Quakers, including William Penn. Of the 120 first purchasers of properties in West Jersey, more than one-third had suffered imprisonment or fines for their Quaker convictions. Although there was talk of creating a religious refuge in West Jersey, it is clear that this purchase was financially motivated. Many of these men were land speculators, and few, other than Penn, ever visited—much less set up residence in—America. In order to make the venture as attractive as possible, the new proprietors of West Jersey worked up their own Conditions of Settlement, which included the following:

> [A]s no man, nor number of men upon earth, hath power or authority to rule over other men's consciences in religious matters . . . every such person and persons may have and enjoy . . . the exercise of their consciences, in matters of religious worship throughout all the said province.[7]

William Penn actively recruited settlers for his plantations among the Pietist religious sects of Germany and the Netherlands, whom he had encountered during a youthful tour of the continent. In this he was hugely successful; the eight thousand people who immigrated by the end of 1685 far outnumbered those who came to New England in the great migration of the 1630s.

It was not only the initial grant holders and proprietors who speculated in land. Bernard Bailyn pointed out that land speculation was everyone's work and it affected everyone, for it was a natural and rational response to two fundamental facts of American life: the extraordinarily low ratio of people to arable land, and the strong likelihood that the ratio would change quickly and radically as the population grew. Every farmer with an extra acre became a land speculator—every town proprietor, every scrambling tradesman who could scrape together a modest sum for investment.[8]

Large tract owners often employed agents in Europe who worked with shipowners in the Netherlands and in England to entice young men, particularly craftsmen who had completed or nearly completed their apprenticeship, to come to the colonies, where they could work off their passage and the cost of a parcel of land over a period of four or five years.

The direct consequences of the Concessions and Agreements and the speculative fervor are noteworthy: New Jersey was one of only four colonies (including Rhode Island, Delaware, and Pennsylvania) that did not adopt a state religion, so it became a haven for a number of dissenting and persecuted sects—Scotch-Irish Presbyterians; English Quakers; Welsh Baptists; German, Swiss, and French Protestants—a diversity reflected in the state throughout the following century.

This was not the "melting pot" sort of diversity to be found in New York, however; it appears that West Jersey, in particular, consisted of a number of small ethnic enclaves—Scotch-Irish in Monmouth, Dutch in New Brunswick and Somerville, German Protestants in sections of eastern Hunterdon, English Baptists in the region north of Trenton, and Quakers throughout Burlington. Each brought its own religious tradition, language, and culture, which were largely maintained until the Great Awakening in the 1720s and 1730s broke down many of the barriers between the various groups. Whereas New England and Virginia were to remain ethnically homogeneous for several generations, New Jersey was ethnically diverse in the extreme. "Settlement advanced without central organization or control, creating a mosaic whose pattern was formed simply by ease of routes of access, accidents of land claims and the contours of the terrain."[9]

Rare is the New England church that sits isolated, a few miles from the nearest village. The Puritan church was the essence of the New England town; it was its government and the author of all rights, including the right to reside in the town. Although many settlers from New England brought that orientation with them when they landed in Salem, Gloucester, Monmouth, and Essex, for example, the Puritan model did not long obtain here, except in Newark, and some communities did not build their first church or meetinghouse until twenty years or more after initial settlement. Newark, Middletown, Shrewsbury, Woodbridge, and Piscataway were exceptions; they were purchased and settled by groups of New Englanders who immediately laid out towns.

The seventeenth-century proprietors and their agents, who looked out

FAIRMONT METHODIST EPISCOPAL CHURCH

over vast stretches of open land purchased from the Indians, were in it for the money. They sold large tracts to friends and to other speculators, who, in turn, sold to settlers, mainly for farms. With a few notable exceptions like William Penn and the colonists of Newark, they were not interested in founding colonies or establishing plantations like the early Dutch in the upper Hudson valley. Land was an asset, to be turned over to creditors in the payment of debts, or to be subdivided and sold off to farmers, who would pay annual "quitrents," as they had in England, as well as the initial purchase price.

The proprietors of East and West Jersey emphasized county government—local courts were needed to settle minor land disputes—so as early as 1699, the colony was divided into eight counties. The counties, in turn, were divided into townships, most of which had no distinct center. Thus, New Jersey developed in a very different manner from New England. Much of the colony consisted of clusters of widely scattered farms and a few hamlets. The population of the entire colony in 1699 has been estimated at less than twenty thousand.[10]

Location

FARMERS IN THIS REGION had little need for a town; they wanted a wholesale market or transportation to get their produce to one. Growth of the towns along the Delaware River owed much to the ready access to Philadelphia, as did the towns in Bergen and Hudson to New York. Greenwich, Salem, Mount Holly, and Bridgeton developed as transportation centers or ports of entry because they were sited on navigable creeks that allowed sailing vessels well inland. It is not surprising, then, that the hamlet, an "unincorporated, haphazardly arranged collection of houses, a shop to two, perhaps a blacksmith shop or the shop of some other craftsman and a church building,"[11] not the town, was the most common population concentration in much of the colony during the first hundred years following initial settlement. Where there was water power for a mill or two, a town was likely to develop, but, with the exceptions noted, that was not the principal pattern in the colony.

With the high mortality characteristic of the period, the first public institution to be located was generally a burial ground. This was often established by the religious core of settlers, particularly the Quakers, but just as often it was a farmer who set aside an acre for Christian (meaning Protestant) burials. A small plot of land adjacent to the burial ground was frequently donated as well, but devout settlers might meet in private homes for years before a church or meetinghouse was built. Early church records show that many of the plots on which the churches and meetinghouses were built were leased for "one peppercorn, to be paid annually on Easter Sunday, if demanded," with the actual transfer of title taking place even a generation later. Usually the donor granted land for a specific church, but occasionally the grant was simply to a "Christian" church, meaning not Catholic, particularly in areas settled by Reformed, Lutheran, and Presbyterian adherents, who seemed to have less preference for a particular liturgy than for the language of the clergy. In one case, the land was deeded to a Presbyterian church, but the trustees were required to extend "liberty to the ministers of the Low Dutch Calvinistical [Reformed] persuasion to preach and perform divine services therein at such times as there is no religious worship performed by the above congregation."

GRAVE MARKER,
READINGTON REFORMED CHURCH

Location of the parsonage also followed a different pattern than in New England, where a good, centrally located lot with ample farm land (the *glebe*) was provided in the initial town plan. Except in the Quaker settlements, which had no preacher, and in Newark and a few of the other Puritan communities, the minister was expected to raise crops for his table, as he was paid a paltry sum, which would not have been sufficient for his needs and that of his family unless he grew his own food. The parsonage was generally, but not invariably, located adjacent to the church; of course, ministers who served several congregations, which was the norm even well into the nineteenth century, might be located central to several but adjacent to none. The glebe was usually purchased for the benefit of the minister, who had a life right to it, and might be located anywhere in the general vicinity.

So in much of New Jersey the earliest churches were found in hamlets and in remote areas that were equally convenient (or equally inconvenient) to a widely scattered population. Whereas the typical New England town had a single center, the focus of religion, trade, and habitation, the rural neighborhood of the middle Atlantic colonies had several. Sometimes a crossroads store stood beside a church meetinghouse, but often the religious centers of the area were several miles removed from the business district.[12]

There are two reasons for this widespread pattern in western and southern Jersey. The density of settlement was still low, even at the time of the Civil War, so a central location was important; most church members need travel only two or three miles, and no one would have to travel more than, say, six or eight. Perhaps equally important was the availability of free or cheap land. Farmers and craftsmen had little cash until well into the early decades of the nineteenth century, but were often willing to donate their time, and even some land, for a community purpose. The land might not be especially convenient, but it was free.

The tavern and the post office—particularly where the tavern keeper also held office as the postmaster, as was fairly common late in the eighteenth century—not the church, were more likely to serve as the hub of community life in the Scotch, Dutch, and German settlements. Rum and hard cider were considered staples (workmen, even those engaged in building a church, often received part of their compensation as a daily ration of rum or cider). Widely scattered parishioners needed a place to gather and socialize between the morning and afternoon services (which generally lasted several hours each), so it would have been common to find a church and tavern in close proximity. Indeed, a number of families withdrew from the Amwell Presbyterian Church in Hunterdon County in 1797, not over doctrinal differences, but because they wanted a place of worship closer to their homes and also because there was no tavern nearby wherein they might refresh themselves. They built a new church across the road from a tavern in Flemington.

Within the larger towns, the earliest churches are indeed found on the village green, at the major crossroads, or at a prominent, near central location. That was true not only for the planned towns of Newark and Shrewsbury, for example, but for virtually every town. A good clue to the nationality and religion of the earliest settlers is the denomination of the church nearest to the center of town. That does not hold for Catholic churches, which arrived much later and had to buy their way into prominence, but it is a useful rule of thumb for other sects. It is unusual in Salem, Cumberland, and Burlington not to find a Quaker meetinghouse near the center of the early towns; in Hunterdon, Middlesex, and Somerset, not to find a Reformed, Lutheran, or Presbyterian church at the center; or in Bergen not to find a Reformed church on what was once the village green. If the original settlers came from New England, the odds are you will find a Presbyterian church in a prominent place in the center of town. The corollary also holds: if you find a Quaker meetinghouse near the town center, even in the northern areas of the state, as in Plainfield and Shrewsbury, chances are that Quakers were among the earliest settlers, if not the founders of that town.

A Catholic church near the center does not have similar significance; Catholics arrived in large numbers in most of the state sometime after 1840, so the location of a Catholic church in a prominent place, as in Camden, Jersey City, Trenton, New Brunswick, and Lambertville, simply means that the land was purchased and the church built long after the founding of the town. In the case of Lambertville in Hunterdon County, the land had to be purchased by a couple of sympathetic Protestants and later deeded to the Catholic church because the prominent site on Bridge Street across from the Baptist church would simply not have been sold to Catholics.

New Jersey does not have many towns with a village green or commons remaining, but if we specify a central location on the dominant street, a short

First Reformed Church, Hackensack

list of towns with churches built by the founding settlers and located there would include Basking Ridge, Bloomfield, Caldwell, Elizabeth, Freehold, Hackensack, Morristown, Newark, Somerville, Woodbridge, and Woodbury, to name a few. Later arrivals had to settle for locations a street or two removed from the center of town, and Catholics and blacks in the early to mid-nineteenth century built even farther out. As Methodists and Catholics moved into the mainstream, economically and socially, they bought land nearer the center of town or in the better neighborhoods; presence, more than convenience, was the reason.

By the 1870s and 1880s even modest-sized cities hosted dozens of churches, several serving ethnic enclaves that might be only a few square blocks in size. St. Peter's (now Queen of Angels) in Newark served a German Catholic population concentrated a half mile west of the center of town; St. Bridget's in Jersey City, well away from Journal Square, served an Irish neighborhood; St. Stanislaus in Trenton served a Polish population concentrated in that area of the city. The Chambersburg section of Trenton contains

St. Columba Catholic Church, Newark

at least a half dozen ethnic Catholic congregations (most from middle Europe and most in churches built in the early part of the twentieth century); similarly, the town of Roebling in Burlington County has several national brands of Lutheran and Catholic congregations. Churches not only dominate the neighborhood, they also mark ethnic denominational affiliations clearly recognized by residents. Thus, the proliferation of churches in the cities is at least partly explained by the ethnic and cultural identity they provide.

In rural areas it was the long distances that prompted so many Methodist and Baptist churches to be built in the days when most parishioners walked to services. Horses were needed for farm work and few farmers had wagons, so conveying the family to a church located three or more miles away was a Sunday ordeal. The several horse sheds that remain behind churches and meetinghouses in Hunterdon, Burlington, and Salem Counties, for example, were built well into the nineteenth century, and even then, the number of stalls would not have been sufficient had each family possessed a horse and

St. Stanislaus Catholic Church, Trenton

carriage or wagon. Walking was the primary means of getting to church, and not for religious reasons, as with some Jewish sects in which the devout may not ride on the Sabbath. In rural counties like Cumberland, Hunterdon, Salem, and Warren, the typical solution to the problem of a seven-, eight-, or

BETHLEHEM BAPTIST CHURCH RUIN

more mile walk was to form a daughter church, frequently treated as a mission, closer to home. Some congregations serving scattered early settlements in time spun off so many daughter churches that they were left with too few members to continue. The Bethlehem Baptist Church, the stone ruins of which are visible from Interstate 78 in Hunterdon County, sponsored daughter churches or dismissed members to congregations in Clinton, Lebanon, and Cherryville, all three to six miles away.

If one could not be on the commons, corner lots were favored in the cities (more so than in the smaller towns and hamlets), so the oldest churches, or the wealthiest, usually occupy a corner, whether in the city proper or out in a residential area of single-family homes. Several of the architectural pattern books issued after the Civil War urged Episcopal congregations to locate land where the chancel could be oriented to the east, and to buy enough land to cover the church's capital or operating costs through the sale of cemetery plots.

Where the population was small and consisted of a number of nationalities, a Union church might be erected and the pulpit shared by several itinerant ministers, as in Finesville and Long Valley along the Musconetcong River in Warren County. Once a denomination had enough members, they often withdrew from the Union congregation and formed their own church.

Construction

MOST OF THE SURVIVING churches from the eighteenth century are second-generation churches and meetinghouses, the first generation being a log structure. Of the forty-five eighteenth-century churches I have surveyed, twenty were built of stone, seventeen of brick, and eight are braced-frame wooden buildings; virtually all succeeded an earlier log or frame building. With one exception, the Quaker meetinghouses were built of brick or stone; the early Baptist, Anglican, and Presbyterian congregations apparently built with whatever they could afford, as there are examples of each type for each of those sects.

It is too easy a generalization to say that stone buildings predominate where Dutch and Germans settled, the English preferred brick, and a congregation only built with wood if they could not afford stone or brick. A bit of explanation may be useful regarding the types of construction during the early colonial period to about 1800.

Log Construction

All denominations have left records indicating that their earliest churches were log structures; some a little more elaborate, with a small gallery or even a wooden floor, but, from the descriptions of early clergymen, they were rudimentary. Many were soon replaced, but others served for many decades. No log churches have survived. There were several hexagonal and octagonal buildings, some log and several of stone, but they long ago disappeared.

Following the log structures, buildings erected for religious purposes fell into three categories: (1) Quaker meetinghouses were essentially domestic in scale and design, a one- or two-story dwelling with an entry—usually two doors—on the long side and an interior stairway to the gallery. (2) Presbyterian, Reformed, and Baptist congregations in the smaller towns built considerably larger rectangular meetinghouses, rather like Dutch and English town halls of the period. The entrance was usually on the long wall, opposite the pulpit, and internal staircases led to galleries that extended along three sides of the church. (3) In the urban areas, which were few, by the end of the eighteenth century there were large rectangular churches with an imposing tower at the gable end, in the manner of the Wren-Gibbs churches in London, but much simpler in ornamentation. The first two would not have required special architectural knowledge or sophisticated construction skills, but the latter certainly would have.

Stone Construction

Stone would have been a familiar building material to most of the early immigrants; a number of masons, carpenters, and other skilled craftsmen are listed as early settlers, especially in Quaker areas. The stone was quarried locally or gathered from the fields. It may have been squared and dressed, but that represented a great deal of labor, so dressed stone was usually reserved for the front of the building; the other three sides were left rough. The Presbyterian church in Deerfield exposed two sides to the public, so the best stones gathered from the surrounding area were used for the front and the east side of the church, along the public road. Where the stone had been squared off and dressed, it was laid up in regular rows; fieldstone was uncoursed, and often stuccoed. In the late nineteenth century, architects employed carved and textured stone; Romanesque-style buildings made extensive use of roughly dressed or rusticated stone surfaces. A few of the pattern books written for Episcopal congregations on building a church advised the use of stone on the grounds that a wooden building advertised the fact that the congregation could not afford to build with stone.

BRICK

Compared to stone, brick was a more expensive and labor-intensive building material in the eighteenth century. Bricks were often made of local clay and

AMWELL METHODIST EPISCOPAL CHURCH

First Baptist Church, Bordentown

fired on site or nearby. Church records frequently noted the name of the contractor/builder, the number of bricks to be procured (about forty thousand for a medium-size church), and the cost of the materials. By the end of the eighteenth century, brick was increasingly used in urban churches and often required by municipal code because of the hazard of fire. Wood could yield finer detail than stone or brick, of course, so when a higher style was desired, as we see in several of the early Georgian buildings, wood rather than stone was used for the door and window surrounds, the cornice, and the steeple or belfry.

Wood Construction

Except for the Quaker meetinghouses, the second church erected by a congregation was usually a wood-frame building, often built without nails, and covered with plank siding or shingles. Wood can be remarkably durable; the shingles on the oldest part of St. Peter's Church in Freehold, built in 1751, are original. Buildings of the highest quality employed very heavy timbers, some weighing far more than even two or three men could lift. They assembled the walls on the ground and tilted them up into place, exactly as one might have done with a barn or large dwelling. "The entire raising operation crackled with danger because at any moment a lifting pole or poles might snap or a makeshift fastening break and an entire subassembly—or the whole half-finished structure would crash down, crushing men and boys."[13]

The materials and construction methods influenced the kinds of buildings that were erected, particularly as most congregations did not employ an architect. Although some labor was often performed by the parishioners, especially on the simpler churches, records from the period indicate that a carpenter and/or mason were usually engaged, and often a contractor or builder as well. Under the circumstances, builders tended to stay within traditional forms and methods. The similarity to raising a barn is instructive:

OLD TENNENT CHURCH, NEAR FREEHOLD

(LEFT) PATTERN-BOOK DRAWING OF A GOTHIC CHURCH BY J. COLEMAN
(RIGHT) ST. MARY'S CHURCH, BURLINGTON

Raising [a reinforced-frame building] retarded innovation and made work scarce for architects. Every husbandman laying out the sub-assemblies around the floor of his barn understood that his neighbors would devote one day to raising them into position. It was impera-tive, therefore, that he plan a barn immediately familiar to everyone because no one had time to discuss an unfamiliar construction. Builders frowned on novel designs not only because raising them took more time but because they proved dangerous. Raising sub-assemblies imperiled all helpers even when everyone . . . understood them perfectly; raising a strange frame tempted ·fate. By the early eighteenth century, therefore, frames in each of the great colonial regions had been standardized, and builders kept them standardized until the middle of the nineteenth century.[14]

But by the early decades of the nineteenth century, pattern books were available, illustrating how to plan and construct Greek Revival, neoclassical, and Gothic designs for dwellings and public buildings, including churches. By midcentury, every builder was familiar with several of these books, including those by Asher Benjamin, Minard Lefevre, and Richard Upjohn, and many of the more prosperous congregations regularly engaged a professional architect.[15]

Architects, Master Builders, and the Use of Pattern Books

THE ARCHITECTURAL PROFESSION in the English-speaking world is hardly older than the American colonies. Inigo Jones, who designed buildings for King James in the early part of the seventeenth century, might properly be said to be the first professional English architect. Christopher Wren, who rebuilt most of the London churches after the fire of 1666, was a self-taught architect, as was Peter Harrison, the first American architect, who designed several Federal-style churches in Boston just before the Revolutionary War. Harrison was a businessman who learned architecture from the books by Wren, James Gibbs, Jones, and Palladio. It is not surprising, therefore, that most of the early churches in New Jersey did not employ an architect in their design and construction. Indeed, the earliest churches were, as I have noted, simple log cabins, but when the settlers were well enough established to consider building a more appropriate house of worship, the engagement of an architect was rarely a possibility on this side of the Atlantic.

The early records of Jersey churches are fairly sparse in their details of design and construction, but it is clear that most relied on a master builder or supervisor to carry out a roughly sketched concept. A notable few, however, recorded the name of the architect. Sometimes it was the minister who designed the building, occasionally a member of the church, as was the case for Trinity Church in Newark, where a ship captain and parishioner, Josiah Jones, is recorded as the architect. Robert Smith, a leading Philadelphia architect, responsible for the design of Carpenter's Hall and several churches in Pennsylvania, was the architect for both Christ Church in Shrewsbury and St. Peter's Church in Freehold. Seventy years later the practice of church building had become specialized enough in New Jersey to support a contractor who apparently did nothing but build and erect steeples.[16] But so prevalent was the practice of contracting with a local builder to carry out a rough concept that as late as 1885, books on church architecture, written for the parish committee and minister who were about to undertake a new building, were warning of the dangers of failing to employ an architect in the design and oversight of construction.[17]

In too many instances the erection of the parish church is directly undertaken by the priest of the parish, or by a parishioner, aware of his incapacity in matters of church architecture, when presumption has not the better part, but forced by circumstances, in his view of the case, to undertake a commission of such vital importance to the spread of Christianity and to Architecture as an art. . . . It is not an uncommon proceeding for parishioners to apply to better skilled artists, at a distance, for their design, when the erection of a church is projected, and console themselves with the false idea that they have all that is required for so holy an undertaking when inspecting the voluminous rolls of designs transmitted to them.[18]

In church architecture colonial builders were clearly dominated by the ideas prevailing in the homeland, but the Reformation and the persecutions in Europe had brought about a revolt against the ecclesiastical architecture of Rome as well as against the Catholic religion. The high Anglican Church style was predictably rejected by Puritan and Quaker, but also by most Reformed sects as well. The upshot was that the earliest churches were exceedingly plain by our standards.[19] Since the pulpit, not the altar, was the center of Reformed Protestant worship, it was important to seat as many people as close to the pulpit as possible, which is why many of the early

INTERIOR, LOCKTOWN BAPTIST CHURCH

churches, like the Reformed church in Neshanic (Somerset County) and the Presbyterian church in Greenwich (Warren County), were much wider than their European counterparts, had a shorter nave, and invariably had a gallery along three sides. Like the early Puritan meetinghouses, many churches were square, or nearly so, and many rectangular churches had their pulpits in the middle of the long side—an arrangement that disappeared in all later remodelings.

Until the rise of the Greek Revival style in the 1830s and the Gothic Revival a decade later, the design of many Jersey churches reflected the New England origins of many of the settlers. There are no Dutch churches, no German churches, no French Huguenot churches in New Jersey; the eighteenth-century buildings are mostly regional adaptations of English traditions. Even where the Dutch and German influence was strong and clearly seen in homes and barns, ecclesiastical buildings quickly moved toward English styles in design and construction. Quakers built as they had in the English midlands, and most everyone else in the northern part of the state built a meetinghouse like the Presbyterian church in Springfield or a traditional church like the Old First Church in Elizabeth. The early Dutch Reformed churches in Bergen County, built around the time of the Revolution or just after, differ only in details from the Presbyterian churches in Newark and Bloomfield. In South Jersey the meetinghouses of the Baptists, Lutherans, and Presbyterians are essentially English buildings in construction and in detail. Their plan resembles that of a Georgian townhouse or town hall more than a religious structure.

It is clear, however, that a few Anglican priests and bishops were more

OLD PILESGROVE PRESBYTERIAN CHURCH, DARETOWN

ORIGINAL ST. MARY'S EPISCOPAL
CHURCH, BURLINGTON

ambitious. The oldest surviving church in the state, St. Mary's Episcopal Church in Burlington, is an exceptional example of colonial Georgian architecture; not high style by English standards, but clearly conceived as appropriate to a provincial capital. Old Swedes in Swedesboro, designed by its well educated, Swedish-born pastor, who was very familiar with the churches of London, is another example.

By the end of the eighteenth century, the drawings of Palladio, Inigo Jones, Christopher Wren, and James Gibbs were well known in the colonies, and there are several surviving examples in New Jersey of churches based on Wren-Gibbs designs (such as Old First and Trinity Episcopal Churches in Newark), although it appears that several of these designs were adapted from New England churches. Congregational (now Presbyterian) churches in Newark, Bloomfield, Elizabeth, and Rahway appear to be derived from the Old North Church in Boston, which was built in 1729–30. The scale of these buildings would present the only challenge to the builder, as the individual details had already been worked out for a generation or more. From the records, it appears that most of the work was done by men and boys from the congregation; a builder or supervisor is occasionally mentioned, but no architect. The advocates (generally the minister) for these buildings did not have to make a choice between Greek Revival, neoclassical, or Gothic, as the range of styles thought appropriate for a house of worship was constrained by a rejection of popish or High Church (Anglican) concepts. Beyond that, the "design" was probably little more than specifications of dimensions and the quality of the materials.

Distinct from modern practice, where you get the blueprints and stick to them, colonial plans changed as the work progressed. The building committee [often along with the pastor] wrote up specifications, but specifications such as "neat and plain" are wide open to

OLD SWEDES CHURCH, SWEDESBORO

interpretation. When the committee started putting in windows . . . they quickly fouled up any overall architectural theme.[20]

On the other hand, many of the early carpenters were more than craftsmen; immigrants themselves, they had worked on a variety of buildings back home, and were able to assist the building committee. The pastor of Old Swedes in Delaware recounted the construction of that church in 1699: "Now the carpenters, ready to set up the roof timbers, came to him with the suggestion that the appearance would be greatly enhanced by building up the gable end."[21]

A century and a half later, the approach was different when the building committee of the First Presbyterian Church in Trenton was faced with replacing the old stone building they had outgrown—"after thorough study and visits to several other churches, the plans for the building were decided upon and Nelson Hotchkiss of New Haven, Connecticut, was engaged as the architect."[22] Some contracts called for the presence of the architect on site, but in smaller parishes, the committee often simply bought a set of plans and contracted with a builder. Plans for St. Patrick's Roman Catholic Church in Newark were prepared by the church's own priest,[23] which was not uncommon even in the middle of the nineteenth century.

By the time of the Civil War, church leaders and the public had become so aware of architectural styles that most congregations either engaged an architect or bought a set of plans. Some pattern books went through multiple editions, and architects were regularly writing new volumes of advice for ministers and congregations contemplating a building project.

Francis Parker, in his book entitled *Church-Building*, wrote, "As to the order of architecture, it is not worth while to throw away time in discussion which shall be adopted;

First Presbyterian Church, Trenton

that question has practically been settled in favor of the Gothic. The Protestant sects [Parker was writing for an Episcopal audience] and the sect of the Jesuits should be allowed the monopoly of classic and renaissance architecture."[24] He proceeded to cover the location of the church and the amount of land that should be acquired (he recommended establishing a substantial cemetery because the sale of plots could fund the church operations for years), materials (stone, if possible), as well as plans for the several parts of the building, and he cautioned against proceeding without the on-site supervision of an architect.

Additions and Renovations

VERY FEW OF THE churches and meetinghouses that survive have not been enlarged or remodeled. Most have electricity, heat, and plumbing, of course, but the modifications have usually gone well beyond that. In many cases, the original congregation would not recognize the church in its present state.

> Congregations build when they must and when they can. They must build when they reach a certain size and have no other place to meet, such as the time of first settlement or when a building burns to the ground. More remarkably, people appear to build, or structurally modify their buildings whenever they can. . . . [V]irtually no unmodified examples of American church buildings are to be found. No sooner did the paint or mortar dry, than did someone in growing congregations begin thinking about the next building project. Thus countless churches built in the meetinghouse style soon added bell towers, even in the south where churches at crossroads were too far from farms and plantations to have any utility.[25]

Growth in membership and an expansion of the functions the church was expected to perform were the most common reasons for modification. Congregations often added 12–15 feet to the rear of the building to accommodate a larger membership. A basement might be dug, or a wing added to house a Sunday school or provide meeting rooms, for the church was often the locus of a community's social and political life as well. "A congregation in 1830 engaged in little except worship, pastoral care, and mission; by 1900, a fully functioning church included sports teams, literary clubs, and organized groups of every sort."[26] A schedule of activities for a Methodist church in

Hunterdon from 1863 shows several dozen activities—meetings of temperance societies and youth leagues, lectures, and social and secular activities—that kept the church open every day and most evenings of the week. Moreover, the rising affluence created a desire on the part of many urban congregations for more room and even an elegance that they might expect from the local opera house. "The facilities that congregations required at the beginning of the Victorian period were minimal and straightforward. There had to be a main sanctuary, of course, and a smaller 'lecture hall,' or chapel for prayer meetings. It is common to have a 'session room,' or deacons' room where board meetings could be held, and perhaps a pastor's study unless this was provided in the manse."[27]

REFORMED DUTCH CHURCH OF CLOVER HILL

In the Episcopal Church from the 1850s through the next several decades, churches were extensively reconfigured to add a chancel and a transept, to change the pulpit and altar, and to effect other physical changes that had liturgical implications. The ecclesiology movement originated in England and urged Anglican churches to reject the pagan Greek Revival style as inappropriate for Christian worship in favor of a return to a pure Gothic as exemplified in the English parish churches of the fourteenth century. Bishop Doane, a leading proponent of the ecclesiology movement in New Jersey, believed that church design was an essential element of the Episcopal liturgy. It was certainly at his urging that most of the Episcopal churches in the state built after 1850 followed the English Gothic model, and that many of the earlier churches were remodeled to incorporate the precepts of the ecclesiology movement. St. Peter's in Freehold, Grace Episcopal (now Church of the Epiphany) in Orange, and Christ Church in Belleville were dedicated by Bishop Doane, then modified a few years later to add a chancel, transept, and other interior elements to bring them into closer conformance with the principles of ecclesiology.

I have noted the date and nature of any exterior modifications and renovations in the pages that follow. Enlargement of the church, often without disturbing the facade, was most common, but in many cases the building was given a complete facelift, as was the Baptist church in Manasquan, which makes the exterior totally anachronistic with the date of erection. The enlargement of the Old North Dutch Reformed Church at Schraalenburgh (in Dumont, Bergen County) was accomplished by taking stone from the rear to extend the sides, then using brick for the new rear, but few congregations are so respectful. The remodeling of the Lutheran church in Oldwick (Hunterdon County) involved moving the door, pushing out walls, and changing the roof and the windows, but parishioners still consider it the oldest Lutheran building in the state. The Reformed church in Clover Hill (Somerset County) added about 20 feet to the front and a new facade, all totally at odds with the original building. The Evesham Friends meetinghouse in Mount Laurel shows evidence of at least two additions and one demolition.

Many congregations started over after tearing down the old

EVESHAM FRIENDS MEETINGHOUSE,
MOUNT LAUREL

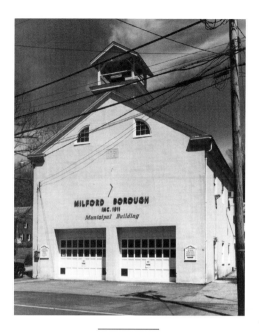

ORIGINAL MILFORD METHODIST
CHURCH, NOW THE MILFORD FIREHALL

church, but in several cases, the old (frame) building was sold, dismantled, and carted off. There is a small Greek Revival building in Little York (Hunterdon County), built in 1844, that uses the frame of a Presbyterian chapel built a few miles away in 1802. Many churches used materials from earlier buildings. The Dutch Reformed church in Hackensack has a number of inscribed stones from an earlier church in its front wall, which members paid to have placed there. Other churches sold the original building and had it moved down the block or across the road so they could rebuild on the original site. In Hunterdon County alone, there are two city halls, a fire company, a bed-and-breakfast, a theater, a couple of manufacturing facilities, and a half dozen residences that were originally churches.

Architectural Styles

I HAVE NEITHER THE intention nor the knowledge to prepare a primer on architectural styles, but there is a need here to sketch out quickly a few common terms that are used to describe church architecture; "Victorian" or "Gothic" simply will not do for any but the most casual observer. From the architectural style we can infer the era when the church was built (or remodeled). Because there is a relationship, sometimes a very strong relationship, between the elements of the architectural style and the denomination, we need to be attentive to design as well as to construction and location. Architectural style is usually meant to include the plan (rectangular, cruciform); the location, shape, scale, and symmetry of the basic elements, such as entrances, windows, towers, columns, pediment, buttresses, pinnacles, and gables; the door and window treatments; and other decorative elements and textures, such as shingles and rusticated or carved stone. I have avoided a synopsis of the history of American ecclesiastical architecture, but I cannot avoid the architectural vocabulary and so must include a basic description and a few representative examples, which will serve as an orientation for the photographs.

QUAKER MEETINGHOUSE

The meetinghouse style is a square or rectangular plan (never cruciform), usually one or two stories, with a gable roof and a balanced principal elevation containing, usually, two entrances. It may be as small as a standard dwelling or perhaps very large, capable of seating several hundred people. A Quaker meetinghouse is sparely ornamented and would never be mistaken for a traditional church because of the absence of any obvious ecclesiastical elements, such as pointed-arch windows or a steeple. Quaker meetinghouses show little variation in style, even down to the profile of the benches and the dimensions of the posts supporting the porch roof.

BURLINGTON FRIENDS MEETINGHOUSE

Georgian or Federal Meetinghouse

The Presbyterian, Reformed, and Baptist meetinghouses are usually two-story rectangular buildings, generally symmetrical, and often embellished with classical detail. They are built of wood, brick, or stone. In the earliest examples, the door is as likely to be on the long side as on the gable end, or

Old Broad Street Presbyterian Church, Bridgeton

they might have doors on three sides, as do the Cohansey Baptist and Old Broad Street Presbyterian Churches (Cumberland). The door surrounds may be elaborate, as they are on the Blawenberg Reformed Church (Somerset), and the pediment and cornice occasionally embody classical details. The building might have a belfry, as do Old Tennent (Monmouth) and Springfield Presbyterian (Union), but rarely a tower or steeple.

Schoolhouse

Because small, often Methodist, churches are so common, and yet have so little in common with other styles except for the occasional display of Gothic windows or a belfry, I have chosen to use the term *schoolhouse* as a style rather

Faith Fellowship Chapel, Burleigh

than simply call these buildings "vernacular" architecture. The schoolhouse is a small building, often a single story and not much larger than a residence, although the size of the windows and their arrangement would suggest that it is not a dwelling. It is likely to have its entrance in the gable end, which fronts the street, and it might have a belfry and even Gothic and/or stained-glass windows, but otherwise is sparely ornamented.

Wren-Gibbs Neoclassical

The traditional church of the mainstream Protestant sects consists of a large rectangular building with a tower aligned with the axis of the nave; the tower is often surmounted by a belfry and/or a steeple. There is usually a well defined pediment, and the tower might interrupt the pediment or be free-standing. The entrance is often through the tower, although triple doors are common, and the principal elevation presents a symmetrical facade. The building would be of wood, brick, or stone. Interior stairs lead to a gallery, usually on three sides. This proved to be a very adaptable style, used in both large city churches and small rural ones. In Connecticut the ornamentation

(LEFT) OLD FIRST CHURCH, NEWARK
(RIGHT) POTTERSVILLE REFORMED CHURCH

is likely to be lavish, but most New Jersey churches of the 1790–1825 period are spare. The basic plan was popular into the 1870s, with Gothic and Romanesque window and door elements and Greek Revival pediments.

GREEK REVIVAL

The defining elements of the Greek Revival style are the symmetrical facade with a low pitched roof, a strong pedimented gable, and a porch or recessed entry with prominent columns or pilasters of the Doric, Ionic, or Tuscan order. The portico (porch) might span the width of the building or merely set off a recessed entrance. Many of the churches have a squat belfry or tower, but some are more elaborate. The exterior is usually painted white or of a light-colored stone or cement.

MOUNT HOLLY BAPTIST CHURCH

Gothic Revival

Beginning in the 1840s, the Gothic Revival was a reaction to the limitations imposed by the Greek Revival; it is characterized by asymmetrical arrangements of entrances, windows, gables, and towers, with an emphasis on gables.

CLINTON PRESBYTERIAN CHURCH

The Gothic, or pointed-arch, window and door surrounds, an element of church architecture for centuries, received new emphasis in this style, as did the use of stepped buttresses, pinnacles, finials, and window tracery. "Gothic revival elements were often appropriated and utilized in combination with features of other nineteenth century styles."[28] Use of natural colored stone was an important aesthetic element., particularly in the Episcopal Church, which took as its model the fourteenth-century English parish church. Prominent architects associated with the Gothic Revival are Richard Upjohn, John Notman, Frank Wills, and William Strickland.

FIRST PRESBYTERIAN CHURCH,
BORDENTOWN

It is useful to distinguish two common Gothic traditions: *Episcopal and Roman Catholic* churches followed a cruciform plan, usually with a long nave and side aisles. An Episcopal church that adhered to ecclesiology precepts would have its chancel and altar at the east end of the nave, and the chancels for both sects would be considerably deeper than for Protestant churches. The large Catholic churches usually adopted the French Gothic style, which tended to be more ornamented than the English Gothic. *Protestant* sects, equating the transept with popery and rejecting the emphasis on the sacraments in favor of the spoken word and audience participation, often dispensed with the transept and aisles, and favored a much shallower chancel or none at all. The building might be almost as wide as it is long, and the amphitheater arrangement of the seating was made possible by a corner entrance.

CARPENTER GOTHIC AND SHINGLE STYLES

Outside of the city, where fire codes made wood construction difficult, some of the leading church architects of the mid-nineteenth century did their most creative work on wooden churches, the plans for which might be offered to a small congregation for as little as one hundred dollars. The

(LEFT) St. Peter's Episcopal Church, Spotswood
(RIGHT) First Presbyterian Church, Cranford

Carpenter Gothic style is usually associated with board-and-batten construction, scrollwork in the fascia boards, and decorative treatment of entrances and belfries. The shingle style is generally associated with the northeastern seacoast, and is characterized by continuous wood shingles and rounded turrets. It was regarded as a fashionable style for architect-designed residences, and so tended to be used by congregations that wanted to announce a presence.

Romanesque Revival and Italianate

This confluence of styles is characterized by rusticated or carved stone decorations; overlarge rounded-arch entrances, window surrounds, and moldings; and decorative arcading beneath the eaves. The plan is rarely rectangular, but complicated, often built around an amphitheater arrangement for worship. Window and door openings are varied in size and placement; towers, turrets, and eccentric chimneys or exaggerated columns can usually be found. The tower is most likely to have a low or flat roof, and contrasting colors and textures are a trademark. H. H. Richardson is the architect most closely associated with this style, which was popular in the 1880s. Provincial churches were

Methodist Church, Trenton

HOLLAND PRESBYTERIAN CHURCH

prone to adopt the round-arched windows, mixing them with elements from other styles.

VERNACULAR

I use the term *vernacular* for churches that have utilized elements of a well defined style, but without an apparent understanding of the design principles underlying the style. That does not imply poor design, but rather a mixing of elements from different styles, such as Romanesque door or window surrounds on a building with a Greek pediment and pilasters. Often the design elements are correctly used, but the proportions are awkward. Many of the steeples in Hunterdon County could be called vernacular although on the whole the churches exhibit a coherent style.

Conclusion

WITH THE EXCEPTION OF the Spanish colonial and adobe traditions, all the major American styles of architecture are represented in New Jersey. Until the 1840s regional styles and building traditions reflected nationality, region, and sect, but with the introduction, first of the Greek Revival and then of the ecclesiology movement's advocacy of English Gothic, regional differences were generally obliterated. Quaker remained Quaker, but their building period was essentially over by the Civil War. Catholic churches were Gothic, following French and German models particularly, then increasingly reflected the middle European national styles of the countries the immigrants came from, which was accentuated in the first decades of the twentieth century.

> The mid-Atlantic region, an area that has historically been known for its cultural diversity, might more appropriately be described as a region of regions. The material expression of this cultural variety is still visible in the range of building methods and traditions that survive. Although much of this variation is due to building type and function as well as geographic situation and the local availability of certain materials, much also results from initial settlement patterns and prevailing building practices.[29]

Rising affluence led to larger and more elaborate churches, although simple vernacular buildings continued to be built, especially by the Methodists and the African Methodist Episcopal (A.M.E.) and other black churches.

.   .   .

I HAVE CHOSEN TO cluster the churches into three large regions representing reasonably distinct early settlement patterns. The Hudson River counties of Bergen, Essex, and Hudson, together with Union and Morris, were settled initially by Dutch moving across the river from New Amsterdam and by Puritans moving in from Connecticut and New England. The Raritan River was a convenient route inland for the Scotch-Irish Presbyterians, the English, and the Dutch settlers coming from Long Island as well as directly from Europe. We should therefore expect to see similarities in the Reformed churches of Bergen and Somerset, but differences between the churches built by the Puritans and those of the Presbyterians and the Germans who flowed into Hunterdon by the 1720s. Burlington on the Delaware River was settled by Quakers coming directly from England, as were many of the towns of Camden, Gloucester, Salem, and Cumberland Counties. This area was soon to be influenced by the culture and architecture of Philadelphia rather than New York or New England, and so we should expect to see a churchscape that is different, not only in the presence of the Quaker meetinghouses, but also in the churches of the Baptists and Presbyterians, who also came early to this region.

County boundaries offer convenient lines to divide cultural influences and building patterns, but occasionally those boundaries must be ignored or fudged a bit; county boundaries were not firmly fixed until well into the nineteenth century, in any case. So in grouping churches together to illustrate the patterns of the churchscape, I have occasionally taken a church out of its home county and placed it in a cultural tradition more akin to that of its earliest members.

No county in the state could serve as a reliable microcosm of the whole in the way that pollsters and demographers often point to a community, especially around election day, as "representative" of the country. There is too much religious and architectural diversity from one region to another. I come to this task having completed a photographic inventory of all the surviving eighteenth- and nineteenth-century churches in Hunterdon, and the conclusions that emerged from that effort have certainly informed this work. Although Hunterdon and Somerset Counties share many commonalities, there are many more Reformed churches in Somerset than in Hunterdon and far fewer Methodist churches. The churchscape of Hunterdon does not look like that of Somerset, Warren, or Morris, although all four have more in common with each other than they do with Cumberland or Salem, for example.

In the pages that follow you will see in the Hudson region, the Presbyterian and Reformed styles yielding to Catholic styles in the mid-nineteenth century; in the Raritan region, the Methodist, Presbyterian, and Reformed churches that dominated the landscape in the early part of the nineteenth century continued to do so as the century closed. In the Delaware region, the Quaker meetinghouse is ubiquitous, but owing to its modest size and setback amidst large trees, it rarely dominates the scene as the later Baptist and Presbyterian churches do. The Episcopal churches are prominent here and there, but many yield pride of place to Presbyterian churches; in any case, they are absent from many areas. The black churches are almost invariably modest in size and located away from the heart of town. None are distinguished architecturally, which reflects the modest circumstances of their founders.

We will look at the churches in chronological order, by region. Although the construction date is given, many of the churches have undergone substantial remodeling and bear only passing resemblance to their original form. In some cases, one has to look at the details, such as the door and window treatment and placement, to get to the original building; in other cases, it is the details that are most interesting.

THE
HUDSON RIVER REGION

TRINITY EPISCOPAL CHURCH
Newark, Essex County, 1742

The original stone church was built in 1742 at the north end of the town's common or militia training grounds, now Military Park. The tower and portico date to 1743, but the remainder of the church, badly damaged during the Revolutionary War, was demolished and rebuilt in 1810. In accordance with the dictates of the ecclesiology movement, the church was enlarged with a chancel and sanctuary in 1857.

TRINITY EPISCOPAL CHURCH, NEWARK

Trinity was the first church organized in competition with the established Presbyterian church in Newark. Although an Episcopal priest had baptized more than five hundred infants by 1740 in a town ruled by the Puritan Church, there was no congregation and no Anglican church until a pillar of that Puritan church, who had been censured by the clergy for doing farm work on the Sabbath, left and started a fund-raising drive to build an alternative church. In 1844 it merged with the Cathedral Chapter of All Saints, which simply meant it gained a bishop's chair. When fire destroyed St. Philip's Church in 1964, its African-American congregation merged with Trinity's; the building is now known as Trinity St. Philip's Cathedral.

CONNECTICUT FARMS PRESBYTERIAN CHURCH,
Union, Union County, 1783

In 1667 several families from Connecticut moved onto good farmland along the Elizabeth River, several miles west of Elizabethtown, which they called Connecticut Farms. They were Puritans, so they worshiped at the closest Congregational church, about five miles away in Elizabeth. For sixty years they made that regular Sunday trek, until in 1730 they decided to build their own church. During that period, the Congregational churches had largely given up their independent status and become affiliated with the Presbytery of Philadelphia, and so the new church, too, was Presbyterian. That church was burned, as was much of the area, by the British in 1780, during their retreat from the lost battle in Springfield. This substantial stone meetinghouse was begun in 1783, but not completed until 1788. Several additions have been made to the church complex, but the original building itself looks remarkably like photos taken more than a hundred years ago.

FIRST PRESBYTERIAN CHURCH
Elizabeth, Union County, 1786

"Old First" is regarded as the oldest English-speaking congregation in New Jersey. It was organized in 1664 by settlers who came from Massachusetts by way of Long Island, and the first building was erected shortly thereafter. Until 1717 it was an independent congregation, which was the New England (Puritan) form of church organization. That meant, among other things, that the residents of the town were obligated to pay taxes to support the minister. In 1717 it affiliated with the Presbyterian Church, largely through the efforts of its minister.

The present building is at least the third on the site and very likely the fourth. Its predecessor, a large frame building, was burned by the British army in 1780, and this one was built in the New England meetinghouse style

CONNECTICUT FARMS PRESBYTERIAN CHURCH, UNION

in 1786. The interior was modified several times, and the church was enlarged in 1851. In 1946 a fire completely gutted the building, leaving only the brick walls standing. The rebuilding was essentially an accurate restoration of the original colonial design.

FIRST PRESBYTERIAN CHURCH, ELIZABETH

PLAINFIELD FRIENDS MEETINGHOUSE
Union County, 1788

This small Quaker meetinghouse might easily be taken for a dwelling. It sits across from what was once the village green, testimony to the role of Quakers in the early settlement of this area. The frame building is shingled; the shuttered windows are traditional Quaker elements, but the dual entrances are missing the usual pent roofs. There are only two other Quaker meetinghouses in the region, in Dover and Summit.

OLD FIRST CHURCH [PRESBYTERIAN]
Newark, Essex County, 1791

Connecticut still marks the Royal Charter that granted that colony's liberties, but since the charter also allowed men who were not members of the Puritan (Congregational) Church to hold office, several families left Milford,

Connecticut, to found a community based on religious principles and governance. Jersey's Governor Carteret offered land and the freedom to worship and govern as they saw fit, so land was purchased from the Indians in 1667, and a new town named Milford was founded. When additional settlers arrived from Connecticut, two avenues were laid out to aid in apportioning land among the people, and a plot at the intersection was set aside for a meetinghouse and burial ground. That plot was diagonally across from where the Old First Church now sits.

Until 1719 the minister was the

head of the church and the town, and, initially, only members of the church were allowed to reside within the town, which stretched as far west as the Watchung Mountains. It was renamed Newark in 1678, to honor the minister, who had been born in Newark-on-Trent in England. The original meetinghouse was built of timber in 1669, and a second one, a squarish stone building with a steeple and bell, about fifty years later.

Although there is no record of a formal decision to end the Congregational form of church-state governance, by 1719, when a Presbyterian minister was hired, it is clear that the Presbyterian Church was in the ascendency in all of the original Puritan settlements in New Jersey. By 1730 there was also an Episcopal church in town, ending the First Church's civic rule.

The construction of this large church was begun in 1787 and appears to be patterned after the Old South Church in Boston. The architect was Eleazar Ball, a name that does not appear in connection with other church buildings.

First Reformed Church
Hackensack, Bergen County, 1791

Although there were a number of Dutch squatters in the area of Hackensack by the last decade of the seventeenth century, the large tract centered around Hackensack was bought by a couple of English traders from the Carib-bean

island of Barbados, who intended to colonize it. They do-nated land for a Reformed church, and by 1694 a congregation was established; by 1696 an octagonal stone building had been erected. That was torn down in 1728 to build a larger one of the same design; in 1790 that was torn down and the present neoclassical stone church erected. In 1869 it was enlarged and the interior remodeled.

Springfield Presbyterian Church
Union County, 1793

This early meetinghouse was rebuilt after the Revolutionary War, when it had been burned by British troops as they retreated through Springfield following their defeat near this site in 1780, the last significant engagement of the war in New Jersey. Although this building was probably not the proto-

type for other churches of the area, for the next thirty or forty years many of those churches followed essentially this same plan. The Reformed churches in Blawenberg and Hillsborough are remarkably similar, as were the Presbyterian church in Woodbridge and the Second Presbyterian Church in Elizabeth, although the latter is built of brick. Details on the cornice of this building have been traced to William Pain's book, *The Practical Builder*, published in London in 1774, but the pattern books of this period left the general plan to be worked out by the builder.

English Neighborhood Reformed Church
Ridgefield, Bergen County, 1793

The location is not the English neighborhood that the Dutch settlers referred to, which was in Leonia, but the stones of the original 1768 church were used to rebuild in 1793 on land donated for a church that would adhere to the Reformed liturgy as laid down in the Netherlands. The sandstone construction used clay mortar, a practice common to the Dutch in New Jersey, but rare outside of Dutch buildings. The style is similar to that of other early Dutch Reformed churches in Bergen County; the steeple and windows are identical to those of the Reformed church in Paramus, built seven years later.

ENGLISH NEIGHBORHOOD REFORMED CHURCH, RIDGEFIELD

(LEFT) BLOOMFIELD PRESBYTERIAN CHURCH
(RIGHT) DUTCH REFORMED CHURCH OF SCHRAALENBURGH, BERGENFIELD

BLOOMFIELD PRESBYTERIAN CHURCH
Essex County, 1797

Formed as a daughter church of the Old First Presbyterian Church in Newark in 1794, which it resembles except for the multitiered steeple, it was originally named the Third Presbyterian Congregation of the Township of Newark. In 1796 the name was changed to honor Major General Joseph Bloomfield, a Revolutionary War hero, and the town ultimately changed its name to Bloomfield as well. Samuel Ward is listed as the architect. Aury King, whose name appears in connection with other churches in the region, was the chief mason. The foundation was laid in 1797, and the first services were held in 1799, although the interior was not completed until 1819. The congregation offered the use of the church to a Baptist congregation in 1851 and a German-speaking Presbyterian congregation in 1855. Additions were made in 1853 and 1883.

DUTCH REFORMED CHURCH OF SCHRAALENBURGH
Bergenfield, Bergen County, 1799

Since 1913 this has been known as the Old South Presbyterian Church, but it began as a daughter church of the Dutch Reformed church in Hackensack in 1724. The congregation was more or less continually at odds with a sister congregation in Dumont and with the Dutch Reformed Church in New Jersey as a whole. That dispute culminated in an affiliation with the Presbyterian Church. This is the second building on the site, erected in 1799; it was enlarged and remodeled in 1866–68. The two front doors flanking the original center one were added, and the side walls were rebuilt to include four windows in place of the earlier three.

OLD PARAMUS REFORMED CHURCH
Ridgewood, Bergen County, 1800

There already were Dutch churches in Hackensack, Tappan, Schraalenburgh, and Dumont when this congregation was formed about 1725. The first building on the site was constructed in 1735. That church was demolished in 1800 as too small, and the present building erected in its place. In design it is very similar to the other Reformed churches in Bergen County, particularly Old South Church in Bergenfield. In 1857 the front was altered with the addition of two new doorways and the porticoes over them, which are also similar to those of the Reformed churches in Dumont and Bergenfield.

OLD PARAMUS REFORMED CHURCH, RIDGEWOOD

Old North Reformed Church
Dumont, Bergen County, 1801

This church makes a pair with the Old South Church—clearly the same architect/builder and style; even the later additions of porticoes over the two doors flanking the tower are similar. Steeple details do differ, and, with its later addition, this is now a somewhat larger building. Originally the two were one congregation, but doctrinal differences led to a split.

Old North Reformed Church, Dumont

Second Presbyterian Church
Elizabeth, Union County, 1821

The growth of the Old First Church through a series of revivals that marked the Second Great Awakening led directly to the founding of this congregation in 1820. Instead of enlarging that building, the congregation voted to allow members to form a Second Presbyterian Church, a decision that was

Second Presbyterian Church, Elizabeth

unusual at the time, as congregations were generally loath to see their financial base weakened by the loss of members to a daughter church.

This building was begun in 1821 and completed ten months later. The building committee stipulated the general area within which the site was to be chosen and decided that the cost of the lot should not exceed two thousand dollars; they settled on a building 60 feet wide and 80 feet long, modeled after Faneuil Hall in Boston. No architect was engaged, but a master carpenter and an assistant were named, as was a master mason and his assistant. The building was enlarged in 1869 and a magnificent amphitheater added at the rear in 1890. There was an adjacent burial ground, but by the 1890s most of the graves had been relocated to Evergreen Cemetery. From old photographs it appears that the entire church was once painted white, the tower and cupola had been a dark brown, and at times most of the front was covered with ivy.

MOUNT FREEDOM PRESBYTERIAN CHURCH
Morris County, 1828

This simple wood-frame building might easily be mistaken for a schoolhouse, as the belfry has no religious aspect, nor do the doors and windows.

MOUNT FREEDOM PRESBYTERIAN CHURCH

FIRST PRESBYTERIAN CHURCH
Rahway, Union County, 1831

Often overlooked in surveys of early churches, this fine example of the Wren-Gibbs school of architecture was founded and built in 1831. The facade was remodeled in a hybrid Gothic-Italianate style in 1876, but the basic outlines are unchanged. Note the particular curve of the arch over the front entrance and how the Gothic windows intersect with the pediment—both unique features in New Jersey.

FIRST PRESBYTERIAN CHURCH, RAHWAY

Emmanuel Methodist Episcopal Church
Springfield, Union County, 1833

This large, meetinghouse-style church is unusual in the placement of its tower, which is normally centered in the middle of the gable end. It sits immediately behind the Presbyterian church in Springfield, and has a small burial ground to the rear.

First Presbyterian Church of New Providence
Union County, 1834

This church is set on a small knoll at a major crossroads. It is a substantial meetinghouse with Georgian door surrounds and steeple. The wooden quoins on the corners of the building and the tower reveal a greater consciousness of architectural style than is evident in the Presbyterian church in Springfield, built forty years earlier, which it somewhat resembles. It was designed by a member of the congregation, one Amos Wilcox. The

(LEFT) Emmanuel Methodist Episcopal Church, Springfield
(RIGHT) First Presbyterian Church of New Providence

congregation was founded in 1739 by settlers moving west from Essex County. It may be that this is the last of the meetinghouse-style churches to be erected in this region, though the style continued to be popular in both the Raritan and Delaware regions for another decade. Originally named the Turkey Christian Church, it became the Presbyterian Church of New Providence in 1778.

OLD BERGEN CHURCH, JERSEY CITY

OLD BERGEN CHURCH
Jersey City, Hudson County, 1839

In 1660 the streets were laid out for the town of Bergen on the hills of the west bank of the Hudson River under an original charter of the Dutch West India Company from 1629. "One of the conditions agreed to by each settler in accepting a village lot was his obligation to contribute to the support of a minister and its schoolmaster."[1] Religious services were conducted by the schoolmaster and *voorlesor* (reader) in private homes until the first Reformed church was built in 1680; a second was erected in 1773. By 1841 that building was too small, so it was put up for bid and sold, at which time construction of the present building was undertaken. The dimensions are 68 feet wide by 84 feet long, and the building is stone, except for the columns, which are stuccoed brick. Embedded in the wall are the cornerstones from the two previous churches.

ST. PAUL'S EPISCOPAL CHURCH
Rahway, Union County, 1843

This very fine building was designed just before the Episcopal Church had fully embraced the English Gothic style as the only appropriate model for an Anglican church. It is a restrained early Gothic design, with oversized Gothic windows in front and small pinnacles at the top of the square tower. It has much more in common with Christ Church of Middletown, built in 1835, or even with the Reformed churches of Bergen County, built almost seventy years earlier, than it does with any of the Episcopal churches built in the region after 1843.

SECOND REFORMED DUTCH CHURCH
Newark, Essex County, 1848

Designed by William Kirk in 1848, the church originally looked similar to the Pottersville Reformed Church in Somerset County (although that church was erected many years later). The building was purchased in 1890 by the Catholic Archdiocese and renamed Our Lady of Mount Carmel, but services were discontinued in 1972. In 1978 it became a Latino cultural center. Recently restored, it is now the Centro Evangelistico da Igreja Assembleia de Deus.

ST. PATRICK'S PRO CATHEDRAL
Newark, Essex County, 1849

By the 1840s the influx of German Catholic and Irish immigrants was substantial and within a few years sufficient to support a second Catholic church in the city. The decision was made to buy land nearer the center of town, and

SECOND REFORMED DUTCH CHURCH, NEWARK

in 1846 construction was begun. The priest from Saint John's actually drew up the plans for this French Gothic church. It is 130 feet long and 70 feet wide, in marked contrast to the mainstream Protestant churches of the period, which were almost as wide as they were long. With its 200-foot-high steeple and prominent location, the church signified that Catholicism had a legitimate presence in the city. Until the erection of the Basilica of the Sacred Heart at the end of the century, St. Patrick's was the designated cathedral church of the bishop of the Newark Diocese.

ST. MARK'S EPISCOPAL CHURCH
West Orange, Essex County, 1850

St. Mark's "represents the beginning and the end of the ecclesiological style in the United States."[2] The church was begun in 1827, well before the Gothic Revival swept the country, "yet the tower, spire and interior of the nave and chancel must have been rebuilt later, when the English influence was at its height. The assurance and competence of the design suggest it was Notman,

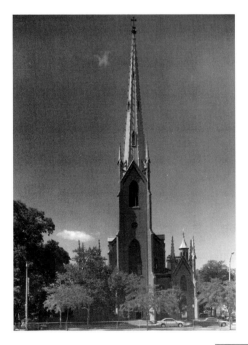

(LEFT) ST. PATRICK'S PRO CATHEDRAL, NEWARK
(RIGHT) ST. MARK'S EPISCOPAL CHURCH, WEST ORANGE

Priest or Upjohn who completed the building. . . . The style was to continue, but the capacity to excite and educate had passed. The Romanesque and Italianate manners the ecclesiologists so much disliked and feared had arrived."[3]

HOUSE OF PRAYER
Newark, Essex County, 1850

Newark's third oldest Episcopal church, organized in 1849, the building was designed by Frank Wills, a prominent architect and one of the leading lights of the ecclesiology movement. This is one of the earlier churches built after the precepts of English Gothic design were enunciated and began to be accepted in the 1840s. The contract with the architect specified that the entire work should be executed under his immediate supervision.

HOUSE OF PRAYER, NEWARK

First Congregational Church of Chester
Morris County, 1851

Nine more Greek Revival churches were built in 1851 with this same plan, excepting only a few details and the occasional substitution of Doric capitals for the Ionic shown here. There were many more Greek Revival buildings in this region at one time, but most were torn down to make way for larger Gothic churches. New Point Baptist Church in Newark is one of the few others remaining. First Congregational is now affiliated with the Presbyterian Church.

First Congregational Church of Chester

HIGH STREET PRESBYTERIAN CHURCH
Newark, Essex County, 1852

This exceptional specimen illustrates the move toward Gothic, and particularly English Gothic, about the mid-nineteenth century. John Welch was the original architect, but the firm of Carrere and Hastings was responsible for the significant rear addition and much of the stained glass. The congregation merged with that of the Old First Church in 1926, and in 1944 sold the building to the African Methodist Episcopal Church. It is now known as St. James' African Methodist Episcopal Church and was recently restored.

SOUTH PARK PRESBYTERIAN CHURCH
Newark, Essex County, 1853

A pair of classical towers, or *tempiettos,* flank the entrance, which is all that remains of this unusual variation on the Greek, or perhaps Roman, Revival style, erected in 1853. The architect was John Welch. Lincoln spoke from its

HIGH STREET PRESBYTERIAN CHURCH, NEWARK

steps in 1861, and the church had a reputation as a progressive congregation. From 1974 to 1989 it was the Lighthouse Temple, providing food and shelter for the homeless. Although it burned in 1992, the building is featured in several survey books on American architecture.

SOUTH PARK PRESBYTERIAN CHURCH, NEWARK

DUTCH REFORMED CHURCH OF SOUTH RIVER
Belleville, Essex County, 1853

This is one of the old congregations of the region, organized by 1697. Legend has it that the steeple on the church built in 1720 was used as an American 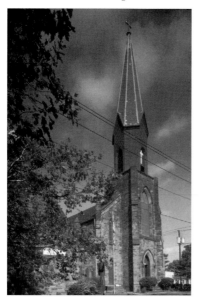 lookout during the Revolutionary War. The current building, the third on the site, was designed by William Kirk, who was also the architect for the Second Dutch Reformed Church in Newark's Ironbound district and the North Reformed Church on Broad Street in Newark, neither of which have much in common with this design. Although in the Gothic mode, traces remain of the traditional Dutch Reformed churches of Bergen County, built fifty years earlier. The cemetery holds the remains of sixty-seven Revolutionary War veterans, more than any other site in the nation, who far outnumber the active parishioners.

CHURCH OF THE MADONNA
Fort Lee, Bergen County, 1854

One of the early Catholic churches in the state, it was built by Jacob Reilly between 1850 and 1854, and was owned by the Reilly family until 1890. It was the first church to serve the Catholics living in Bergen County. The entire building, including the steeple, is constructed of basalt quarried at the nearby Palisades.

ST. MARY'S ROMAN CATHOLIC CHURCH
Newark, Essex County, 1857

The parish was founded by German Catholics in 1854, and this, their second building, was erected three years later. It is a large, red brick building in the German Gothic manner, which is actually close to the Romanesque in the multiple rounded-arch windows and low-pitched roof. The architect is

CHURCH OF THE MADONNA, FORT LEE

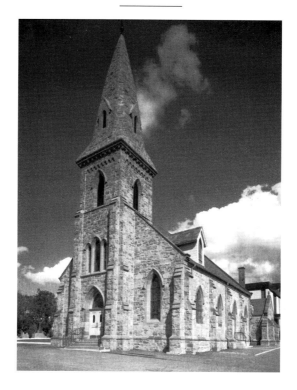

ST. MARY'S ROMAN CATHOLIC CHURCH, NEWARK

unknown, but was clearly versed in the tradition of the Benedictine monasteries. The church is now known as St. Mary's Abbey and is affiliated with St. Benedictine's Preparatory School.

This is a lovely building that is hard to appreciate fully because it sits amid so many other relatively large buildings. Renaissance builders often erected the more monumental churches away from the medieval center of town to permit a proper viewing distance, but in this case, the city has engulfed the church, and the tower no longer dominates the skyline as it did a hundred years ago.

NORTH REFORMED CHURCH
Newark, Essex County, 1858

The variegated stone spire of this fine Gothic building, erected a couple of years after the congregation was organized, exemplifies one of the principal tenets of the Gothic Revival—the use of natural materials of varying colors

NORTH REFORMED CHURCH, NEWARK

and textures. William Kirk, who also designed the Second Reformed Church in the Ironbound section of the city, was the architect. Fires damaged the church in 1922 and 1931.

St. John's Episcopal Church
Elizabeth, Union County, 1860

Organized in 1706, this church was the center of loyalism in the area during the Revolutionary War. The rector, a Reverend Chandler, left for England in 1775, but his family remained and his son became a captain in the New Jersey Volunteers, a loyalist force. Chandler returned to the church following the war it. This Gothic church was built on the site of the original in 1860. The interior is a magnificent example of English Gothic design.

St. John's Episcopal Church, Elizabeth

TRINITY CHURCH
Woodbridge, Union County, 1860

In contrast to the large city cathedral, such as we see in St. John's in Elizabeth and St. Peter's in Morristown a number of years later, the ecclesiology movement prescribed a different kind of church for the rural Episcopal parish, and Woodbridge's Trinity is representative of a style that can be found elsewhere in Jersey. The congregation was formed by 1698; two earlier churches were built on this site. The bell cote, transept, entrances, chancel, and east-oriented altar are characteristic of Episcopal churches built in the state after about 1850.

TRINITY CHURCH, WOODBRIDGE

St. Peter's Roman Catholic Church
Newark, Essex County, 1861

This church was built about a half mile west of the downtown area by a German Catholic congregation with financial aid from the Society for Propagation of the Faith, as were many of the early Catholic churches in the state. It has been known as Queen of Angels since 1930. The Germans have long since left; the church now serves a largely black and Latino congregation.

Lafayette Reformed Society
Jersey City, Hudson County, 1863

If you can look beyond the painted red brick and the aluminum-and-glass front door, you will see a traditional Wren-Gibbs design but with arched door and window surrounds. Founded by a Reformed congregation as a Sunday school in 1816, the church has now passed to a Spanish-speaking congregation and is called the Iglesia Christiana Fuente de Salvacion.

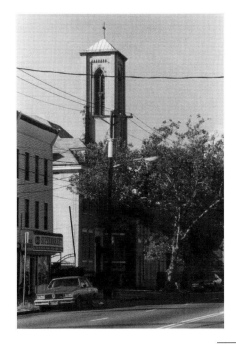 

(LEFT) ST. PETER'S ROMAN CATHOLIC CHURCH, NEWARK
(RIGHT) LAFAYETTE REFORMED SOCIETY, JERSEY CITY

FIRST REFORMED DUTCH CHURCH
OF BERGEN NECK
Bayonne, Hudson County, 1866

This is the oldest church in Bayonne, founded in 1828 and built in 1866. The design is a traditional one, similar to that of the Simpson Methodist Church in Perth Amboy, though of wood and with a much taller spire. The church is now known as the First Federated Church and calls itself Presbyterian-Reformed due to a merger with the Third Reformed and Christ Presbyterian Churches in 1952.

FIRST REFORMED DUTCH CHURCH OF BERGEN NECK, BAYONNE

First Baptist Church
Elizabeth, Union County, 1868

This fine Romanesque church set in what was once an upscale suburban area might easily be mistaken for a Catholic church. The contrasting glazed brick trim, false arcade, and large rose window are more common in Catholic than in Baptist churches of the period. The building is essentially unchanged since it was built in 1868, except for the loss of the Empire-style top to its large tower and another columned tier to the smaller tower. The congregation was not founded until 1842, which is curious since Baptists were among the earliest settlers in nearby Monmouth County.

First Baptist Church, Elizabeth

CLINTON AVENUE REFORMED CHURCH
Newark, Essex County, 1870

This highly decorated Gothic Revival church was built in a once exclusive downtown neighborhood now known as Lincoln Park. Today it houses the Iglesia Roca de Salvacion congregation. Of the several Reformed congregations that once flourished in Newark, only the North Reformed remains.

CLINTON AVENUE REFORMED CHURCH, NEWARK

St. Patrick's Roman Catholic Church
Jersey City, Hudson County, 1870

St. Patrick's was founded in 1870, one of eight new Catholic churches built in the twenty years following the Civil War to serve the rapidly growing, largely Irish Catholic population of the city. Prior to 1854 the Catholic population was less than two hundred, only twenty-four of whom were property owners,

St. Patrick's Roman Catholic Church, Jersey City

the rest being servants. The floor plan is typical of Catholic churches of the period, with the nave extended to more than three times its width. Begun in 1870, the building took almost seven years to complete.

TRINITY EPISCOPAL CHURCH
Elizabeth, Union County, 1871

Now known as St. Elizabeth's, this was the fourth Episcopal church founded in the city. The original building was a small frame structure, but that was sold in 1865, and services were held in the Third Presbyterian

TRINITY EPISCOPAL CHURCH, ELIZABETH

Church until a chapel was built on this site in 1869. This is one of the few small rectangular (rather than cruciform) Episcopal churches built after 1860. The decorative bands of contrasting brick are also somewhat unusual in an Anglican church.

CHURCH OF THE HOLY INNOCENTS [EPISCOPAL]
Hoboken, Hudson County, 1871

Built by the Stevens family in mourning the loss of a young child, this chapel does not appear to be in active use. The building was begun in 1871 and

CHURCH OF THE HOLY INNOCENTS, HOBOKEN

dedicated four years later, but was still unfinished by 1884. The architect, Edward T. Porter, was said to have modeled it after a specific English Gothic church in London, but that identification has been lost. The interior has no pews, which is common in cathedral churches but unusual in a parish church. The Stevens family wanted a church that would be free (with no pew rents, which were standard practice among Anglican churches) and modeled on the churches built in poorer sections of the great English cities.

CHURCH OF THE HOLY ASSUMPTION, MORRISTOWN

CHURCH OF THE HOLY ASSUMPTION
Morristown, Morris County, 1872

The oldest remaining church in Morristown, it is located several blocks away from the green, a short distance from St. Peter's Episcopal Church, which was built in an affluent residential neighborhood many years earlier. It is a substantial red brick building with contrasting trim of Ohio sandstone in the French Gothic style. L. J. O'Connor was selected to draw up the design and plans for the church.

CENTRAL PRESBYTERIAN CHURCH
Orange, Essex County, 1872

Founded in 1869, the congregation hired T. A. Roberts of Newark as the architect for this Gothic building, which was erected on Main Street in 1872. It borrows elements from several Gothic traditions. The building now houses the Faith Fellowship Cathedral.

CENTRAL PRESBYTERIAN CHURCH, ORANGE

First Reformed Church of Orange

Essex County, 1875

This church was founded in 1875 and built that same year. Unusual for a Reformed church, it was constructed on a cruciform plan, with the tower at one of the reentrant angles. It is now the Faith Temple No. 1 Free Will Baptist Church.

First Reformed Church of Orange

OUR LADY OF GRACE
ROMAN CATHOLIC CHURCH
Hoboken, Hudson County, 1875

This large French Gothic building, the largest church in New Jersey at the time, took about three years to build, from 1875 to 1878. It exhibits many elements of the medieval Gothic churches, including the rose window and the very elaborate front entrance treatment.

OUR LADY OF GRACE ROMAN CATHOLIC CHURCH, HOBOKEN

First Presbyterian Church of Caldwell
Essex County, 1875

The area was initially settled by Dutch families before 1720, but they were squatters and could not get a deed from the royal governor, so were displaced by settlers moving out from Newark in the 1740s. It was not until 1770 that there were enough people to make up a congregation; in that year ninety acres were purchased in the village, and an additional fifty acres for the glebe. A frame building was erected by 1793 after determining that they could not

First Presbyterian Church of Caldwel

afford to build one of brick. When fire destroyed it in 1872, a building committee visited various churches and consulted with a few architects. James Carpenter was selected as the designer of this commanding building at a major intersection in town.

St. Mary's Roman Catholic Church
Plainfield, Union County, 1875

The contrasting colored stone in the round arches above the windows is one of several elements that mark this fine example of the French Gothic Revival. The dormers in the roof just above the eaves, the steep pitch to the roof of the tower, and the contrasting horizontal bands are typical of late-nineteenth-century Catholic churches from the Mid-Atlantic states through the Midwest. The church was founded in 1846.

St. Mary's Roman Catholic Church, Plainfield

East Baptist Church
Elizabeth, Union County, 1882

The church was reorganized in 1880, and this frame structure, capable of seating four hundred people, was built in 1882. The L-shaped plan was popular among Methodist and Baptist churches of the period, as it permitted an amphitheater seating arrangement. The church is now known as the Iglesia de Dios Pentecostal.

East Baptist Church, Elizabeth

ADAS EMUNO SYNAGOGUE
Hoboken, Hudson County, 1883

The oldest synagogue in the state, and one of only seven surviving synagogues from the nineteenth century. Built in the Romanesque style, it currently serves as a church.

ADAS EMUNO SYNAGOGUE, HOBOKEN

PRINCE STREET SYNAGOGUE, NEWARK

NORTH BAPTIST CHURCH, JERSEY CITY

PRINCE STREET SYNAGOGUE
Newark, Essex County, 1884

This Moorish-style synagogue was about to be demolished in 1993 to make way for a housing development when it was saved at the last minute. It was built in 1884 for the Oheb Shalom congregation, the second oldest Jewish congregation in Newark. In 1911 the Adas Mishnayes congregation took it over, then sold it in 1939 to the Metropolitan Baptist Church, which held services there until 1993. The Moorish style is rare, but was used occasionally in the latter decades of the nineteenth century in Europe and America. Efforts are being made to preserve and restore the building.

NORTH BAPTIST CHURCH
Jersey City, Hudson County, 1885

Only the facade and the next-door chapel of this substantial Baptist church remain intact. The roof over the nave is missing, and only the lower half of the side wall still stands. The tower and entrance combine Gothic, Romanesque, and Italianate elements.

ST. PETER'S EPISCOPAL CHURCH
Morristown, Morris County, 1887

This church on South Street was organized in 1827, although visiting Episcopal priests had occasionally preached in the area as early as 1763. A New York architect, Henry Cogdon, was engaged to draw up plans for a new church in 1882; he did so, but the plans were never acted upon, and three years later in a competition, McKim, Mead and White of New York won the commission. Charles McKim had recently been in England and had studied a number of parish churches there. The building committee obtained photographs of the interiors of several English churches, specifically including Lichfield Cathedral, which provided the model for the choir stalls and the screen. The church was begun in 1887, but it took twenty-seven years to complete. Halfway through construction, the nave was lengthened, requiring a much larger tower to keep the proportions right; McKim stayed with the project throughout. A long wooden shed was erected on the property; at one end eighteen stone cutters worked during the cold months, and at the other, two blacksmiths continually sharpened and repaired the stone-cutting tools.

ST. PATRICK'S ROMAN CATHOLIC CHURCH
Elizabeth, Union County, 1887

The parish of St. Patrick was organized near the docks about 1857. The area soon had a residence, parochial school, sisters' house, and lyceum hall, and in

1887 the foundation for the present church was laid. It succeeds an earlier church built in 1858. The style is high Gothic, very reminiscent of Cologne Cathedral. This is a substantial church; the interior dimensions of the nave are 90 feet wide and 180 feet long. Each of the twin towers houses three clocks. Immediately above the front entrance is a blind arcade, and above that a large rose window. The previous St. Patrick's Church, just north of this building, now serves as the high school auditorium. The changing demographics of the area have led to a much smaller congregation today, with the number of services much reduced.

HOLY CROSS ROMAN CATHOLIC CHURCH
Harrison, Hudson County, 1888

This exceptionally large church was founded as St. Pius Church in 1863, serving a largely Irish, Polish, and Italian population. Today it conducts services in English and Portuguese. It was named Holy Cross when the current building was completed in 1888.

St. Peter's Episcopal Church, Morristown

Holy Cross Roman Catholic Church, Harrison

PEDDIE MEMORIAL BAPTIST CHURCH
Newark, Essex County, 1888

The only nineteenth-century Byzantine-style church in the state, this massive Baptist church was built in 1890 at a major intersection. It was named to honor Thomas Peddie, a philanthropist and mayor of Newark in the 1860s. The architect was William Halsey Wood.

PEDDIE MEMORIAL BAPTIST CHURCH, NEWARK

SEVENTH DAY BAPTIST CHURCH
Plainfield, Union County, 1890

The Seventh Day Baptists have only a few churches in the state, mostly in South Jersey, but this congregation has been in Plainfield since 1838. Their second church, a large Italianate structure built in 1866 and now used by the Board of Education, sits adjacent to this magnificent building, designed by O. M. Teale.

While I was photographing this church, several passersby remarked that its roof once had imported red tiles and the building is not the same since they were replaced. In fact, the tiles were made in upstate New York and all ninety tons of them are stored in the church's basement. The roof was leaking and the intricate plaster tracery of the ceiling was in danger, so the congregation had to make a choice. One who has seen the interior has little doubt the right choice was made. This remains a remarkable example of the Romanesque Revival, one of the finest late-nineteenth-century churches in

SEVENTH DAY BAPTIST CHURCH, PLAINFIELD

the state. The main sanctuary is in the form of a baptistry, with the pulpit located to one side, so that parishioners in the overflow section, separated by huge sliding doors, can hear.

ST. BRIDGET'S ROMAN CATHOLIC CHURCH
Jersey City, Hudson County, 1890

St. Bridget's was organized in 1869 and built its first church by 1870. The rapid growth of the area's Irish Catholic population necessitated a new church in 1890. This immense red brick building with contrasting trim occupies a full city block.

FIRST BAPTIST CHURCH, HOBOKEN
Hudson County, 1890

This is a fine example of the Romanesque Revival, with its exaggerated tower, elongated triple windows, and large arched entrances. Its corner loca-

ST. BRIDGET'S ROMAN CATHOLIC CHURCH, JERSEY CITY

tion, scale, and high style convey the presence the congregation wished to project in this city that had once been dominated by the Dutch and Germans, but by the end of the nineteenth century, had witnessed a substantial influx of Irish and Jewish residents. The church is now owned by the Seventh Day Adventists.

FIRST BAPTIST CHURCH, HOBOKEN

CHURCH OF THE HOLY ROSARY
Elizabeth, Union County, c. 1890

The several gables, towers, false buttresses, and pointed-arch windows of this church are typical of the late-nineteenth-century wooden Gothic churches built throughout the country. This Catholic congregation was formed in 1888, a year or two before the church was built at First Avenue and Sixth Street. It is now the Iglesia Bautista Christos Laucia Esperanza.

KNOX PRESBYTERIAN CHURCH
Kearney, Hudson County, 1891

The squarish tower with the multiple rounded-arch windows is a mark of the Romanesque Revival. One source gives 1882 as the date of erection, but the cornerstone says 1891.

KNOX PRESBYTERIAN CHURCH, KEARNEY

CHURCH OF THE IMMACULATE CONCEPTION
Montclair, Essex County, 1892

This Catholic parish was organized by 1856, and the original church on this site was built in that year. This Renaissance Revival church was built in 1892.

CHURCH OF THE IMMACULATE CONCEPTION, MONTCLAIR

CRANFORD PRESBYTERIAN CHURCH
Union County, 1893

This magnificent shingle-style building is one of the outstanding churches in the state. It exhibits the asymmetry, enlarged entrances, and multiple pinnacles and gables characteristic of the later Gothic Revival. The architect was James Carpenter.

CRANFORD PRESBYTERIAN CHURCH

First Presbyterian Church
Morristown, Morris County, 1893

Morristown was settled about 1715, and this congregation was organized in 1733 by parishioners who split off from the Presbyterian church in Whippany. A substantial reinforced-frame church of white oak "cut in the old moon" was erected in 1790; it took two hundred men several days to erect that frame, which was torn down and reassembled as a barn in Passaic County almost one hundred years later. The present Romanesque Revival building, designed by New York architect J. C. Cady, was built in 1893.

First Presbyterian Church, Morristown

St. Lucy's Roman Catholic Church
Hoboken, Hudson County, 1895

No services are currently held in this fascinating church near the entrance of the Holland Tunnel. The style is Romanesque Revival. The tower is of particular interest, and not only because of its great height. In the brickwork are echoes of the medieval towers of northern Italy, while the arcade windows above the front entrance are pure Tuscan.

St. Lucy's Roman Catholic Church, Hoboken

CATHEDRAL BASILICA OF THE SACRED HEART
Newark, Essex County, 1899

The cornerstone for this enormous French Gothic cathedral was laid in 1899, but the building was not completed until 1954. In size it compares to Westminster Abbey and is the fifth largest cathedral in North America. The initial architect was Jeremiah O'Rourke. It sits on the highest point in Newark, which was purchased when the Catholic Church was not permitted to buy land in a more central location near Lincoln Park.

CATHEDRAL BASILICA OF THE SACRED HEART, NEWARK

THE
DELAWARE RIVER REGION

St. Mary's Episcopal Church
Burlington, Burlington County, 1703

This fine Georgian building is the oldest church in the state and has been recently restored. It was organized in 1702, the year the two Jerseys became a royal colony, and the Church of England, while not an "established" church, was certainly favored by the royal governor. Burlington was, of course, first settled by the Quakers and was known as New Beverly, after the city in Yorkshire from which several of the founders had emigrated.

A lot was purchased a few hundred yards south of the center of town, adjacent to a burial ground that had been set aside in 1695, "free for all other Christian people, who shall hereafter be reminded to bury their dead."[1] In the original charter, the church was called St. Ann's, but a later charter names it as St. Mary's. The brick building was enlarged in 1834 with a vestibule and north wing, giving the church a cruciform appearance; the entrance was moved and the brick covered with stucco. The church served as the seat of the Episcopacy of New Jersey until the erection of a new building in 1854.

St. Mary's Episcopal Church, Burlington

The first English Quakers and Presbyterians arrived in this area about 1681. Quaker meetings began as early as 1696, and by 1715 the west end of this building had been completed. The east end was added in 1785.

WOODBURY FRIENDS MEETINGHOUSE

UPPER SPRINGFIELD FRIENDS MEETINGHOUSE

Springfield Township, Burlington County, 1727

Located on an unpaved road several miles from Fort Dix, this small brick building is the third oldest Quaker meetinghouse in the state, after those in Woodbury and Seaville (Cape May County). It is now a private residence.

UPPER SPRINGFIELD FRIENDS MEETINGHOUSE, SPRINGFIELD TOWNSHIP

TRENTON FRIENDS MEETINGHOUSE
Mercer County, 1739

A passerby might mistake this small building for a residence, although one rather out of place in downtown Trenton. It is, in fact, the original Quaker meetinghouse, built in 1739 and enlarged somewhat later. The fan window and the dentils under the eaves are not traditional Quaker elements, however, and are unknown in any other meetinghouse in the state.

BORDENTOWN FRIENDS MEETINGHOUSE
Burlington County, 1740

From the location of this meetinghouse, squarely in the center of town, one would rightly surmise that Quakers were the original settlers.

BORDENTOWN FRIENDS MEETINGHOUSE

Hancock's Bridge Friends Meetinghouse
Salem County, 1756

The first log meetinghouse in this area was built in 1685 on an acre of donated land, but it was on the wrong side of the creek from the greater number of members. As there was no bridge yet, a new building was erected in 1718 on the other side of the creek. In 1753 a more convenient plot was donated, and this meetinghouse was completed in 1756.

Hancock's Bridge Friends Meetinghouse

Evesham Friends Meetinghouse

Mount Laurel Township, Burlington County, 1760

Quakers from Evesham, a borough near Stratford-on-Avon, settled here and organized the first religious services in the area by 1694. By 1698 they gained permission to build a meetinghouse, probably near the site of this building, and were helped by Indians with its construction.

Evesham Friends Meetinghouse, Mount Laurel Township

This later meetinghouse is constructed of Jersey sandstone quarried across the road from the building. Both British and colonial troops occupied a wing (an unusual feature, the outline of which can still be traced in the walls) during the war. A large linear addition was constructed in 1798, later used by the Hicksite Quakers during the schism, which is why the building has three front doors.

OLD PILESGROVE PRESBYTERIAN CHURCH
Daretown, Salem County, 1767

Restored in 1941, this beautiful Georgian building appears authentic and unchanged since it was built in 1767. Presbyterians from East Jersey, Connecticut, and Long Island came relatively late to this region of the colony; the congregation was organized in 1741, although preaching had been sponsored by the Presbytery of Philadelphia since 1720. The red brick contrasts with the grey stone lintels, which are, except for initials and a date, unornamented.

OLD PILESGROVE PRESBYTERIAN CHURCH, DARETOWN

Emanuel Lutheran Church at Friesburg
Alloway Township, Salem County, 1768

There are two traditions of the founding of the Lutheran congregation in this locale: one credits the Swedes who colonized the region about 1640, and the other traces it to Germans working at the nearby glassworks. It is clear that Lutheran services were held very early in this area, as this is the second church on the site. This brick Georgian building was enlarged by about a third in 1868.

Emanuel Luthern Church at Friesburg, Alloway Township

GREENWICH ORTHODOX FRIENDS MEETINGHOUSE
Cumberland County, 1771

Greenwich was founded by settlers from Connecticut seeking more religious freedom. The deep Cohansey River, some two hundred yards from the back of this church, enabled the town to serve as a port of entry for ocean-going

GREENWICH ORTHODOX FRIENDS MEETINGHOUSE

vessels during the colonial period. The first meetinghouse was erected in 1698 on this site, just east of the center of town on its broad main street, although the Friends were organized here as early as 1682. This spacious red brick building is unchanged since it went up in 1771. The building is surrounded by sycamore trees, apparently a Quaker tradition, since there are few meetinghouses that do not have at least a couple of sycamores shading the building.

DEERFIELD PRESBYTERIAN CHURCH
Cumberland County, 1771

The Puritans from Connecticut who settled this area about 1725 formed a Presbyterian Society and built a log meetinghouse in 1737. In 1771 this building was erected, using Jersey sandstone gathered from the local fields in the absence of any nearby quarry. The east and south sides (the front and the side facing the road) display large, well-shaped stones whereas the other two sides consist mainly of irregular ones. There is little ornamentation, inside or out, in keeping with the religious beliefs of the congregation. In 1858 the building was enlarged and radically altered in appearance with the addition of five tall arched windows and a vestibule at the front.

RANCOCAS FRIENDS MEETINGHOUSE
Burlington County, 1772

The first meetinghouse in this area was built in 1703 and described as "primitive in the last degree. . . . The floor was of clay beaten hard and the single window of four panes of bull's-eye glass placed in back of the wall where the elders say provided the only means of light when the door was closed."[2] That building served until 1772, when the present meetinghouse was built in the traditional Quaker style. The date is recorded in lighter colored brick set in the eastern gable.

Deerfield Presbyterian Church

Salem Friends Meetinghouse
Salem County, 1772

This is one of the few Quaker meetinghouses where an architect is known to have been employed. In 1772 the Salem Friends engaged William Ellis of Philadelphia to draw up the plans for this large red brick building set prominently near the main crossroads of the town. Not surprisingly, it is the oldest house of worship in Salem. British troops occupied the building during the Revolutionary War, as they did many of the churches in the area. After the war, court was held here for the purposes of confiscating loyalists' estates.

Chesterfield Preparative Meetinghouse
Crosswicks, Burlington County, 1773

In the center of what would be the village green if this were New England sits a large, two-story red brick building with two entrances on the front and

SALEM FRIENDS MEETINGHOUSE

a single entrance on the other three sides. All the windows have shutters, and the two front doors are sheltered by the traditional pent roofs. Tall sycamores are well spaced on the surrounding grounds. This meetinghouse, one of the most picturesque in the state, duplicates one in Buckingham, Pennsylvania, which members of the building committee visited in 1773. Although most Quaker meetinghouses look very similar at first glance, variations can usually be found in the subtler details; in this instance, the buildings are virtually identical.

MOUNT HOLLY FRIENDS MEETINGHOUSE
Burlington County, 1775

Quakers were the first settlers in Mount Holly, so it is not surprising that the meetinghouse is located near the center of town. However, the present building is not the site of the first meetinghouse, built in 1716, a half mile north on the road to Burlington. The center of town shifted south when the mills were

CHESTERFIELD PREPARATIVE MEETINGHOUSE, CROSSWICKS

built on the river, so when it was necessary to build a larger meetinghouse in 1775, a new plot was purchased. About 40 percent of the population of Mount Holly was Quaker at the time. The walls were raised and a gallery added in 1850.

ARNEY'S MOUNT FRIENDS MEETINGHOUSE
Springfield Township, Burlington County, 1775

In 1743 a group of Quakers made application to hold services during the winter season, which was granted. About thirty years later, they built this stone meetinghouse, which burned twice, although in each case, the stout walls survived. Services are held here only a couple of times a year. The burial ground extends up the slope behind the building.

FAIRTON OLD STONE CHURCH [PRESBYTERIAN]
Cumberland County, 1780

The earliest settlers normally move up the rivers from the coast, so it was natural that when Puritans from New England moved into the area by 1680,

MOUNT HOLLY FRIENDS MEETINGHOUSE

Arney's Mount Friends Meetinghouse, Springfield Township

Fairton Old Stone Church

the Cohansey River was the avenue they traveled. Having worn out two wooden churches, in 1775 the congregation assembled a quantity of stone and wood to build a new church, but the British army seized the materials to build a wharf on the river. Although the country was still at war, the church members pledged money and time again, and by 1780 the first services were held in this building. Regular services ended about 1850, when the congregation built a larger church.

OLD SWEDES CHURCH (TRINITY EPISCOPAL)
Swedesboro, Gloucester County, 1784

About 1636 Swedish colonists settled in the lower Delaware valley in what are now Penn's Neck, Swedesboro, and an area near Wilmington, Delaware. They built Fort Elfsborg south of Salem and encouraged settlement by supplying an ordained Lutheran minister approved by the Swedish crown. They built a log church by 1705, which was to last them eighty years, until this large brick building was begun in 1784 and finished, except for the tower and steeple, two years later. The plans for the building were drawn by the young

OLD SWEDES CHURCH, SWEDESBORO

Swedish minister, who had spent some time in England, and it resembles an English church more than its contemporary "Old Swedes" Church across the river in Delaware. By 1792 the congregation had ended its affiliation with the state church of Sweden and become a Protestant Episcopal church. In 1839 the tower and steeple were built, and significant changes were made to the interior, probably to conform more closely to the Episcopal liturgy.

BURLINGTON FRIENDS MEETINGHOUSE
Burlington County, 1784

In 1677 Burlington was settled by two groups of Quakers, one from London and another from Yorkshire, who must have outnumbered their London brethren, for they named the town New Beverly. They soon built a frame meetinghouse, but found it was too cold for use in winter, so they built a brick addition that could be warmed. That structure served as the site of the Yearly Meeting before Philadelphia became the seat of the Friends in America and was also occasionally used as a school and a courthouse. In 1783 a committee of twenty-five was appointed to plan a larger building capable of seating 550 people. The porches were added later, but the building is otherwise remarkably unchanged since it was first erected, including most of the doors, iron latches, and window fasteners.

Woodstown Friends Meetinghouse
Salem County, 1785

The original frame building was built in 1725 and known as the Pilesgrove Monthly Meeting. The date of this building is prominently proclaimed in lighter colored brick. I suspect the extended porch is not original, but replaced the traditional pent roofs above the doors.

Moravian Church, near Swedesboro
Gloucester County, 1786

The Moravians originally came from Germany and settled in Georgia, but soon moved to Pennsylvania, where they founded the towns of Bethlehem, Nazareth, and Lititz. Missionaries were sent into Jersey, and one volunteered to preach to several of the Lutheran congregations in the region that had been without a regular minister. When the Swedish church discovered this, they immediately sent an ordained Lutheran, but a number of the congrega-

Woodstown Friends Meetinghouse

Moravian Church, near Swedesboro

OLD BROAD STREET CHURCH, BRIDGETON

tion, loyal to the missionary, left and formed a Moravian church in the vicinity of Swedesboro.

Services were held in the Quaker meetinghouse until a log building could be erected, and in 1786 the foundation was laid for the present stone church, which was not completed until 1789, probably because of the difficult economic situation following the war. The congregation declined to the point where the church was abandoned in 1804. In 1807 the Methodists moved in without authorization and were soon evicted, as the "Meeting House was built for a place of serious worship." It was eventually deeded to the Episcopal Church, and in 1948 became the property of the Gloucester County Historical Society.

OLD BROAD STREET CHURCH
Bridgeton, Cumberland County, 1792

Perhaps the finest example of Georgian religious architecture in the state, this two-story meetinghouse was built of bricks fired on the site. Bridgeton was flourishing by the time the church was constructed, so it is not located at the center of town, as was common when Presbyterians founded a community, but on donated land at a major crossroads. Regular services have not been held here for more than a century, but the building is still perfectly maintained.

ADAMS METHODIST EPISCOPAL CHURCH
near Swedesboro, Gloucester County, 1793

The Lutheran minister in Swedesboro noted in 1773, "The Methodists have recently nestled themselves in, and roamed around especially in the woods east of Raccoon among the wild people, who had not for the most part confessed any religion before."[3] The "Old Stone Church," one of the oldest Methodist churches in South Jersey, has walls of native fieldstone more than a foot thick. Much of the interior, including the flooring and the benches, is original.

First Cohansey Baptist Church of Roadstown

Cumberland County, 1801

Irish Baptists settled in the area by 1683, to be followed within a few years by Welsh Baptists, who arrived by way of Massachusetts. Both groups built their own meetinghouses, but decided to join and build a common one about 1714, and in 1741 another larger one. By 1796 the congregation was planning a larger church at a more convenient location, and in 1801 they erected the present building, a substantial two-story Georgian meetinghouse that bears a strong resemblance to the Old Broad Street Church in Bridgeton, about five miles away.

Mullica Hill Friends Meetinghouse

Gloucester County, 1808

The common pattern of the spread of Quaker meetinghouses in South Jersey was a few meetings in private homes, followed by a request to meet on a reg-

Adams Methodist Episcopal Church, near Swedesboro

First Cohansey Baptist Church of Roadstown

Millica Hill Friends Meetinghouse

ular basis, and ultimately, which might mean many years later, to build a meetinghouse. That pattern obtained at Mullica Hill; the initial meeting was held in 1797, and eleven years later this building was completed. It is taller than most of the meetinghouses and has but a single door on the gable end, which is a major departure for one of this size.

First Baptist Church of Woodstown

FIRST BAPTIST CHURCH OF WOODSTOWN
Salem County, 1815

Bricks for this church were made on the site from clay dug in the rear of the building, apparently a common occurrence because the records of several other early churches indicate that bricks were made on site rather than purchased and hauled in. The tower was added in 1882. The exceptionally tall rectangular windows are a fairly common sight in South Jersey, particularly in Baptist and Methodist churches.

NEWTON FRIENDS MEETINGHOUSE
Camden, Camden County, 1828

Camden was initially settled by 1682, which is the year of the first Quaker meetings in members' homes. In 1684 they erected a log building and laid out a burial ground. In 1817 the log building burned and a new brick meetinghouse was erected on Mount Vernon Street. When the split between the Orthodox and the Hicksite factions took place, the Orthodox retained the brick building and the Hicksite group, after a few months of meetings in

NEWTON FRIENDS MEETINGHOUSE, CAMDEN

homes, built a small frame structure in 1828. The latter group prospered and the town of Camden grew up around that building. By 1885 the old frame structure was proving inadequate, but members objected to the cost of building a new one. The design for the subsequent major renovation was probably by Wilson Eyre of Philadelphia. It incorporates his Queen Anne leanings in several details. "Although well within the expected limits of muted expression and simplicity, [this meetinghouse] presents a unique and pleasing variation of the pattern."[4]

ST. JOHN'S EPISCOPAL CHURCH
Salem, Salem County, 1837

A missionary sent in 1722 by England's Society for the Propagation of the Gospel in Foreign Parts wrote, "This part of the county being first settled by Quakers, Quakerism has taken such root here that of all ye weeds of Heresies and Schism, this is by far ye most flourishing. The Quakers are about five times ye number of those of ye Church of England who are about seventy adult persons. Besides Quakers there are no other sort of Dissenters near Salem Town except three families of Anabaptists, and as many independents. I do not know if there is one Papist in ye whole county."[5]

Nevertheless, a church was built in 1728, the only Anglican church between Burlington and Cape May. By the time of the Revolutionary War, the congregation, without a regular minister since 1749, had dwindled and the church, which has been seriously damaged by British troops, was in ruins. Plans were made in 1836 for a new church, and William Strickland of Philadelphia was engaged as the architect. Strickland seems to have worked in a variety of styles—Greek Revival, Georgian, Egyptian, and the English Gothic of this building, which was undoubtedly influenced by Bishop Doane, who dedicated the church in 1838. The plan for this church was adopted essentially unchanged by a parish in Maryland ten years later. The original steeple was dismantled and replaced by this Norman tower in 1962.

St. John's Episcopal Church, Salem

First Presbyterian Church
Trenton, Mercer County, 1839

This very fine Greek Revival building is the third church on the site and includes materials from its predecessor, which was built in 1805. After visiting several other churches, the building committee engaged Nelson Hotchkiss of New Haven, Connecticut, as architect and solicited bids from builders. The walls are stuccoed brick and the columns are poured concrete.

First Presbyterian Church, Trenton

OLD PITTSGROVE BAPTIST CHURCH
Pittsgrove Township, Salem County, 1844

Pittsgrove was a preaching station for the area's Baptist minister in 1730, and in 1743 this became a branch of the Cohansey Baptist Church. Like most early congregations, they met initially in a log meetinghouse, but soon replaced that with a wood-frame building of "good oak hewed timber." In 1844, according to church records, the "substantial old frame was sold to the negroes for a house of worship and evidently removed from the spot, for the same year the Baptist House was erected." This simple brick building, largely unadorned, is impressive in its setting and well maintained.

ST. MICHAEL'S EPISCOPAL CHURCH
Trenton, Mercer County, c. 1844

This curious building was known as the Church of Trenton until a few years after its construction in 1753. The congregation was founded in Hopewell about 1704 and met there until this building was erected on a plot donated by one of the early land speculators in the colony. Like many of the churches, it

OLD PITTSGROVE BAPTIST CHURCH, PITTSGROVE TOWNSHIP

was severely damaged during the Revolutionary War; the Hessian commander quartered troops there prior to the Battle of Trenton. The church was enlarged in 1844 and generally rebuilt in 1871, except for the facade, then altered again in 1886. I have found no information about the original architect or the rationale for the design, which is most unchurchlike.

ST. MICHAEL'S EPISCOPAL CHURCH, TRENTON

ST. ANDREW'S EPISCOPAL CHURCH
Mount Holly, Burlington County, 1844

St. Andrew's was originally a mission church of St. Mary's in Burlington, organized by 1742. This is the third church to be built by the congregation; no architect is mentioned, but a deacon of the Baptist church served as contrac-

ST. ANDREW'S EPISCOPAL CHURCH, MOUNT HOLLY

tor. This substantial building of English perpendicular Gothic design, located prominently across from the courthouse, suggests that the Episcopal Church was able to maintain or rebuild a substantial presence in an area that had been inhospitable to the Church of England during the Revolution. The rector of the church in 1777, a solid Tory, collaborated with Benedict Arnold and Major Andre, and had to flee the country. Services were suspended until 1784, when they were conducted by a Methodist minister.

St. Peter's Episcopal Church
Clarksboro, Gloucester County, 1845

A prominent sign high on the tower proclaims, "Founded 1770"; this wooden building was erected in 1845. It is one of the last of the traditional meeting-house-style churches built by the Episcopal Church in the state.

Chapel of the Holy Innocents
St. Mary's Hall, Burlington, Burlington County, 1845

The ecclesiology movement overwhelmed the Georgian style of religious architecture throughout New Jersey, not only for the Episcopal Church, but eventually for other mainstream Protestant sects as well. This chapel announced the beginning of that movement. Under the direction of Bishop Doane, in 1845 architect William Notman designed an English Gothic church that largely followed the principles laid down by the movement's authorities: a stone building with a transept, Gothic windows, buttresses, and stained-glass windows. The tracery in one of the windows is an exact copy from a church in England. "It is an early example, possibly the first, of the exact reproduction of an English Medieval detail in an American church."[6] The timing is somewhat ironic since it followed by only a few years Ralph Waldo Emerson's call for an indigenous national culture in his American Scholar address. The north-oriented altar was a grave violation of ecclesiological principles, but the overall attempt was applauded by the English critics. Before this building, a crossing (transept) would have been considered too popish, even for the Anglican Church. As Doane was the bishop of New Jersey, he was an influential advocate of the fourteenth-century English Gothic parish church as the only appropriate model for an Episcopal church.

ST. PETER'S EPISCOPAL CHURCH, CLARKSBORO

CHAPEL OF THE HOLY INNONCENTS, ST. MARY'S HALL, BURLINGTON

ST. PAUL'S EPISCOPAL CHURCH
Trenton, Mercer County, 1848

Firmly in the English Gothic style, this building was described in 1883 as "one of the most tasteful and convenient churches in this region." This might well have been true, though the author of that encomium was likely its rector at the time. The church is now occupied by the Iglesia Christiana Domasca, as proclaimed by a banner above the front entrance.

SOLOMON WESLEY METHODIST EPISCOPAL CHURCH
Blackwood, Camden County, 1850

Blackwood was once called Davistown, a black community formed by freed slaves early in the nineteenth century on a parcel of land left in a will by a white slave owner to one of his servants and her family. The Davistown Colored School, which no longer exists, and campgrounds were also established

(LEFT) ST. PAUL'S EPISCOPAL CHURCH, TRENTON
(RIGHT) SOLOMON WESLEY METHODIST EPISCOPAL CHURCH, BLACKWOOD

on the property, which served as the center of the small community, composed mostly of family members. This simple church has recently been restored.

CHURCH OF THE SACRED HEART
Mount Holly, Burlington County, 1852

One of the earliest Catholic churches in the state, the congregation was formed in the late 1840s when a ship from Ireland landed in Burlington and many of the passengers settled in Mount Holly, presumably because of the employment offered by the iron and thread mills, which employed about four hundred workers in 1850. Land was purchased uphill from the mills, and in

CHURCH OF THE SACRED HEART, MOUNT HOLLY

1852 this simple frame building was erected. In 1871 the congregation had grown and the church was dilapidated; still, it was moved to a site on the "sand hill," "an interminable expanse of sand . . . and there were no houses for a quarter of a mile,"[7] where it served until a large new church could be built on the property in 1872. The building was then used as a school.

St. Stephen's Episcopal Church
Mullica Hill, Gloucester County, 1853

In marked contrast to St. Mary's, built the following year in Burlington, this vernacular church is built of uncoursed stone. The windows are Norman or

St. Stephen's Episcopal Church, Mullica Hill

possibly Saxon rather than Romanesque, the cornice might best be described as Carpenter Gothic, and the tower Italianate.

St. Mary's Church [Episcopal]
Burlington, Burlington County, 1854

One of the most important churches in the country, St. Mary's was designed by Richard Upjohn, who followed the plan of a small parish church in England, St. John's Shottesbrook, for which he had measured drawings. The concept of the church was laid out by 1847, and it was largely constructed between 1846 and 1848. The church is considered a landmark, both for its

St. Mary's Church [Episcopal], Burlington

pleasing proportions and because it was "the first attempt to follow a specific English medieval example."[8] St. Mary's is a cruciform church with the tower and spire directly above the crossing. It can seat eight hundred people.

BETHLEHEM AFRICAN METHODIST EPISCOPAL CHURCH
Burlington, Burlington County, 1855

Largely remodeled (in 1873 and again in the 1980s) since its erection in 1855, this is one of the earliest substantial churches built by a black congregation in South Jersey. The A.M.E. Church had been founded in Philadelphia in 1816, and the relatively high rate of manumission in Quaker areas led to the rapid growth of benevolent societies, lodges, and especially churches. This congregation, organized in 1836, was obviously more prosperous than most.

BETHLEHEM AFRICAN METHODIST EPISCOPAL CHURCH, BURLINGTON

FIRST PRESBYTERIAN CHURCH
Salem, Salem County, 1856

By the middle of the nineteenth century there were dozens of pattern books for architects and builders to follow, showing the classical orders of the Greek Revival or the true Gothic. One of the most popular was Samuel Sloan's *The Model Architect*, first published in 1852. Although John MacArthur of Philadelphia was the architect for this building, the likelihood is strong that he followed Sloan's plan for "a village church." Whereas Sloan projected the cost of his design at about $4,800, the Salem committee spent more than six times that, albeit for a substantially larger building and much taller steeple, and that sum included the cost of the lot, horse sheds, and furnishings.

FIRST PRESBYTERIAN CHURCH, SALEM

Broadway Methodist Episcopal Church
Salem, Salem County, 1858

Representative of several churches in South Jersey is this large meetinghouse that combines a number of elements from the Greek and the Romanesque Revivals. The meeting room is on the second floor, leaving the first available for Sunday school and other gatherings, as the Methodist churches at mid-century, in particular, were the loci of every kind of social, educational, and reform meeting, which generally kept them occupied seven days and evenings a week. By this time, the Methodists had escaped from their earlier reputation as undisciplined and disreputable and built this church in a very prominent place on the main street in town.

Broadway Methodist Episcopal Church, Salem

Jacob's Chapel
[African Methodist Episcopal]
Wrightstown, Burlington County, 1859

I believe this is the oldest black congregation in the state, organized in 1813, three years before the founding conference of the African Methodist Episcopal churches in Philadelphia. The building was constructed on land donated by a Quaker in 1859. The property also contains an even older church that was moved to this location.

St. Andrew's Episcopal Church
Bridgeton, Cumberland County, 1859

Well away from the center of town, the site of this Anglican church bespeaks its troubled history. Although some of Bridgeton's earliest settlers were adherents of the Church of England, this was Quaker country, and the later Presbyterian and Baptist immigrants were not attracted to the church that

JACOB'S CHAPEL, WRIGHTSTOWN

had persecuted them in England. In spite of several periods of straitened circumstances and many years without a regular minister, the congregation managed to build this church by 1859, only nine years after the first regular Episcopal services were held in town.

QUINTON METHODIST CHURCH
Quinton Township, Salem County, 1860

By the 1880s most regional and denominational differences in church architecture had disappeared. This Methodist church could easily be found in any small town in Minnesota or Colorado.

MOUNT MORIAH AFRICAN METHODIST EPISCOPAL CHURCH
Mount Holly, Burlington County, 1863

There was a substantial black population in Mount Holly in the early decades of the nineteenth century; they met in private homes and in an old

(LEFT) ST. ANDREW'S EPISCOPAL CHURCH, BRIDGETON
(RIGHT) QUINTON METHODIST CHURCH, QUINTON TOWNSHIP

schoolhouse until a church was built in 1826 on the lot where the burial ground is now located—well out of town. The congregation grew, and by 1861 they built a larger building on the site of the present church, a half mile closer to town. It was destroyed by a tornado in 1863, but immediately rebuilt. This church has a distinctive idiom in the prominence of the stained-glass windows adorning a building that otherwise is more or less indistinguishable from its neighbors in this residential section of town.

Church of the Immaculate Conception
Camden, Camden County, 1864

The first Catholic services in Camden were held in a "poorly furnished room in the old City Hall" sometime in the 1850s.[9] The congregation grew rapidly, and by 1859 they had built a large Gothic church. But the priest was unhappy

Mount Moriah African Methodist Episcopal Church,
Mount Holly

with the building, so persuaded the congregation to buy land and build this one in the English Gothic decorated style at Broadway and Market; the church had moved uptown.

CHURCH OF THE IMMACULATE CONCEPTION, CAMDEN

Deerfield Methodist Episcopal Church
Deerfield Township, Cumberland County, 1868

The modest ornamentation of this simple wood-frame meetinghouse undoubtedly reflects the economic situation of its members. Most of the small towns in West and South Jersey have similar Methodist churches, generally built between 1840 and 1870.

Deerfield Methodist Episcopal Church,
Deerfield Township

Juliustown Methodist Episcopal Church
Springfield Township, Burlington County, 1869

The building is similar to Mullica Hill Methodist Church, built twenty years earlier.

Sacred Heart Roman Catholic Church
Mount Holly, Burlington County, 1872

This is the second church on the property and sits about fifty yards from its wooden predecessor. The original plan for this substantial red brick building by architect Charles Keely included a bell tower, but that was never built.

Juliustown Methodist Episcopal Church, Springfield Township

Sacred Heart Roman Catholic Church, Mount Holly

PROSPECT AVENUE PRESBYTERIAN CHURCH
Trenton, Mercer County, 1875

Although this building has some of the elements demanded of an Episcopal
church by the ecclesiology movement, they are assembled in a different man-
ner and so this Presbyterian church, now home to the Imani congregation, would never be mistaken for an Anglican church. The asymmetrical arrange-
ment of gables, towers, and windows marks this as clearly within the late Gothic Revival tradition. It was built in what was once a prosperous residential area a mile north of the city center; as the population has changed, the church now serves a different congre-
gation—a pattern that is found in all of the state's major cities.

PROVIDENCE PRESBYTERIAN CHURCH
near Florence, Burlington County, 1878

The first impression of this lovely church is that of a railroad station in some
college town. It was built well away from the nearest populated area, Florence, probably to serve a scattered rural population.

BRIDGEBORO METHODIST EPISCOPAL CHURCH
Burlington County, 1880

With its large wood-frame building, this Methodist church dominates the
town, even if the town is small.

PROVIDENCE PRESBYTERIAN CHURCH, NEAR FLORENCE

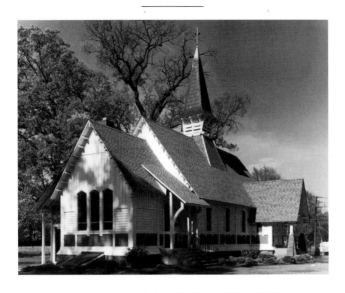

BRIDGEBORO METHODIST EPISCOPAL CHURCH

Avas Achim Synagogue
Norma, Salem County, 1888

In 1882 Jewish immigrants, largely from Eastern Europe by way of New York City, were settled on farms in Salem and Cumberland Counties. Set in a residential area of this hamlet, formerly known as Bradway Station, the building is indistinguishable from a small residence; there is no element that might identify its religious purpose, much less that it is a synagogue.

Avas Achim Synagogue, Norma

Or Yisrael Synagogue

Rosenhayn, Cumberland County, c. 1900

Although the congregation has disbanded, this early synagogue is well maintained. It is set in a remote area, surrounded by large farms and an occasional clutch of small residences. At one time it served the Russian Jewish population that settled in the area just before the turn of the century, now largely dispersed. Only the large Star of David set high in the gable end marks it as a house of worship instead of a small, one-room schoolhouse.

Or Yisrael Synagogue, Rosenhayn

THE
RARITAN VALLEY REGION

ZION LUTHERAN CHURCH
Oldwick, Hunterdon County, 1749

Although much altered since its erection, this is the oldest church in the region and the oldest Lutheran church in the state. The congregation got its start in 1714 when a group of families in the Millstone area of Somerset County attempted to organize a German Reformed (Lutheran) church in the area. It is likely that a couple of log cabin churches were erected in Pluck-

ZION LUTHERN CHURCH, OLDWICK

emin and Potterstown sometime between that date and 1749, when the present stone building was erected in the hamlet of Smithfield in Tewksbury Township. The entrance was originally on the long side, and the building had a hipped roof, typical of early German and Dutch construction. It was extensively remodeled in 1830, 1854, and 1883.

OLD TENNENT CHURCH
(FIRST PRESBYTERIAN CHURCH)
near Freehold, Monmouth County, 1751

One of the most historic churches in the state, it has been known variously as the Upper Meetinghouse, the Freehold Church, the Old Red Church, the

OLD TENNENT CHURCH, NEAR FREEHOLD

Tennent Church (because of the famous Tennent ministers, who preached there), and finally as the Old Tennent Church. The congregation was founded after 1685 by Scottish Covenanters (a Presbyterian sect) who fled the religious persecution in their country in that year. After landing at Perth Amboy, many settled in Monmouth County and by 1692 had built a log church, which became known as "Old Scots Church," at a place called Tope-namas, near what is now Freehold. According to legend, the first meeting of a Presbytery in America was held at that church in 1706.

This building, the second on the site, was built in 1751 in the meeting-house style. In 1778 the Battle of Monmouth, the largest land battle of the war, was fought here, and cannon balls are said to have pierced the walls of the church. It was used as a field hospital for American soldiers following the battle.

MOUNT BETHEL BAPTIST MEETINGHOUSE
Warren Township, Somerset County, 1757

Except for the white clapboard siding, this might be mistaken for a Quaker meetinghouse. Built in the English tradition with separate entrances for men

MOUNT BETHEL BAPTIST MEETINGHOUSE, WARREN TOWNSHIP

and women, the small building has a gallery and raised pulpit. It was organized in 1767, but it is clear from the minutes of that meeting that the meetinghouse had already been built.

FRIENDS MEETINGHOUSE AT STONY BROOK
near Princeton, Mercer County, 1760

Permission to hold worship services, a requirement of the Society of Friends, was requested and granted to a group of Quaker settlers in the Princeton area in 1710. The original meeting was held in a home, but when an eminent Quaker preacher visited in 1725, the meeting was held in a large barn. By 1726, four years after the initial request to build a meetinghouse, a 30 x 34-foot stone building was erected. It served for the next thirty-four years, until

a committee appointed to determine what was to be done with the building decided it needed to be replaced. Built on the foundation of the old one, this meetinghouse was completed in 1760. The only other surviving Quaker meetinghouses in the region are in Shrewsbury and Manasquan.

NESHANIC DUTCH REFORMED CHURCH
Montgomery Township, Somerset County, 1762

The congregation was formed in 1752 and construction began in 1759. Church minutes are unusually detailed and include a list of who worked on the building and the cost of all materials. Construction took 533 man days, not including the time of apprentices, and 73 gallons of rum were consumed, apparently a daily ration as part of the wages. The interior galleries were not completed until 1772. Until 1786 all preaching was done in Dutch; for the benefit of junior members, an English-speaking minister performed the services two Sundays a month. The building is rather wide for its depth, a common feature among Dutch Reformed churches of the period, which were often wider than they were long. The lancet windows resting on the doorways are unusual, although this may have been the original configuration of several of the Dutch Reformed churches in Bergen County as well.

St. Thomas' Episcopal Church
Alexandria Township, Hunterdon County, 1768

In 1723 a missionary from the Society for the Propagation of the Gospel in Foreign Parts (the Church of England's missionary arm) visited the area and wrote that he found the people ready to erect a house of worship. According

NESHANIC DUTCH REFORMED CHURCH, MONTGOMERY TOWNSHIP

to a historian writing a century ago, "the probability is that it was established as a mission enterprise in the days of Queen Anne, who feared the dissenters and Quakers would outstrip the Church of England in the rapid filling up of the country."[1] The first church was either a log cabin or perhaps a frame building because a girder containing mortises and other evidence of such construction were found. This small stone structure was built in 1768, but the interior had fallen into disrepair by the middle of the nineteenth century. It was restored in 1870.

St. Thomas' Episcopal Church, Alexandria Township

CHRIST CHURCH [EPISCOPAL]
Shrewsbury, Monmouth County, 1769

Shrewsbury was one of the first towns in the state to be settled, largely by Puritans from New England. The first Church of England services were held in this area in 1702, shortly after the proprietor's charter had been revoked and East and West Jersey were converted to a Crown colony. Land for the church at the main crossroads of the town, where we find a Quaker meetinghouse and a Presbyterian church as well, was donated in 1706 and the first stone and brick building erected about 1715.

In 1769 plans for a wood-frame building to accommodate four hundred people were prepared by Robert Smith, an architect/builder from Philadelphia and one of the leading church architects of the colonial period. He also designed St. Peter's Episcopal Church in Freehold and Carpenter's Hall in Philadelphia. This is one of the earliest examples of a shingled frame meetinghouse in the state, which was probably the prevailing style for Episcopal churches in this region until the Gothic Revival style began to be promoted about 1840. The tower was added in 1874 and crowned with the cupola that was formerly mounted on the roof.

CHRIST CHURCH, SHREWSBURY

St. Peter's [Episcopal] Church
Freehold, Monmouth County, 1771

The frame of this church was erected in 1771, although the interior was not completed until 1806. It was designed by Robert Smith, a leading architect/builder from Philadelphia. The door, formerly on the long side, was moved to the gable end in 1837, and in 1855 the building was enlarged and the interior considerably altered under the influence of Bishop Doane, who was actively promoting the ideas and design principles of ecclesiology, a powerful movement within the Anglican Church that advocated a return to fourteenth-century English Gothic as the only appropriate architecture for Anglican churches. Another prominent architect, Henry Dudley of New York, was involved in a major reconstruction of the church in 1878.

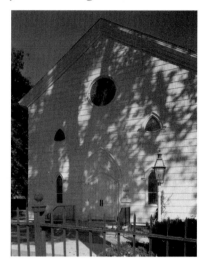

Christ Church [Episcopal]
New Brunswick, Middlesex County, 1773

By the year 1743 New Brunswick had become a town of considerable note and thus merited a prominent Episcopal building, although the Anglican Church was not well regarded in this predominantly Dutch Reformed area. The original church was built about 1750, and the tower and spire were added in 1773; the church was rebuilt in 1803 and the spire in 1813 after being struck by lightning. In 1852 the nave was torn down and rebuilt on a larger scale under the direction of architects Henry Dudley and Frederick Wills.

First Dutch Reformed Church of New Brunswick
Middlesex County, 1812

Early settlement of the area was by the Dutch—some from Albany, New York, as well as from New York City, Long Island, and Connecticut. Initial

Christ Church, New Brunswick

services were held in the area by 1703, and a church was built by 1717, perhaps earlier. The site of the present church was leased to the congregation in 1765 for a term of two thousand years at a fee of one peppercorn, on demand, and in 1767 a square stone structure was built.

This is a large church, one of the largest in the state at the time, built in 1812 to seat 1,100 people. The style is similar to that of the Dutch churches in Dumont and Bergenfield, although the steeple was built in 1827, then remodeled in 1835. In the 1820s the center of the business district was directly in

FIRST DUTCH REFORMED CHURCH OF NEW BRUNSWICK

front of the church; the town fathers felt that a clock visible to the merchants and shoppers was needed, so they appropriated the money to buy and place a large clock in the steeple in 1828.

SHREWSBURY FRIENDS MEETINGHOUSE
Monmouth County, 1816

One of the few shingled Quaker buildings in New Jersey, this is similar in size and design to the meetinghouses in Crosswicks (Burlington County) and Hancock's Bridge (Salem County), although both of those are built of brick, as are most Quaker meetinghouses in the state. Quakers were among the earliest settlers in Shrewsbury; this congregation formed in 1672.

SHREWSBURY FRIENDS MEETINGHOUSE

Second Presbyterian Church of Amwell
Raritan Township, Hunterdon County, 1818

This church was founded as German Reformed in the 1740s, in the midst of an Anglican church to the southwest, a Presbyterian church to the east, and a Baptist church to the southwest; the region seems to have been well churched. It was originally known as the High Dutch Calvinistical of Preisbeterian Church. Its affiliation changed from Reformed to Presbyterian to Reformed and back to Presbyterian by 1810. The large, reinforced-frame meetinghouse style is common throughout the region.

Second Presbyterian Church
Hackettstown, Warren County, 1819

This is the oldest religious structure in Warren County, built after the original church, erected in 1763, was taken down. It has seventy-eight pews, about three times as many as that first building. The Greek Revival portico and

SECOND PRESBYTERIAN CHURCH OF AMWELL, RARITAN TOWNSHIP

belfry were added in 1838, somewhat obscuring the clean meetinghouse style. By 1860 the congregation had grown and a larger church in the Gothic Revival style was erected across the street. The building now houses a Baptist congregation.

LOCKTOWN BAPTIST CHURCH
Delaware Township, Hunterdon County, 1819

A mission church of the Old School Baptist Church in Hopewell, this congregation was organized in 1742 and erected this stone building on or near

SECOND PRESBYTERIAN CHURCH, HACKETTSTOWN

the site of the first church in 1819. The church is not located near any population center, and there are other Baptist churches only a few miles away in Baptisttown and Flemington, so I suspect doctrinal or personality differences influenced the location of this building. The Georgian fan window and door treatment may be a later remodeling, as the Old School Baptist tradition did not admit of such "worldly" vanities.

FIRST PRESBYTERIAN CHURCH
Shrewsbury, Monmouth County, 1821

The church was founded by Congregational settlers from New England before 1727. This unassuming frame building was put up in 1832, immediately east of the Episcopal church. It was enlarged in 1845, and but for the steeple, might be mistaken for a country schoolhouse. The style is vaguely Greek Revival, largely in the pediment, corner pilasters, and door treatment, but the 1820s were still a little early for a full Greek Revival treatment in the smaller towns of the state.

LOCKTOWN BAPTIST CHURCH, DELAWARE TOWNSHIP

OLD SCHOOL BAPTIST CHURCH
Hopewell, Mercer County, 1823

This is one of the few early brick churches in the region. Only its back wall survives from the first church, built in 1747. The congregation was organized in 1712 by former members of the Baptist church in Middletown. The symmetrical or balanced front elevation is basically Georgian, but with very little of the decoration one might normally find in the door surrounds; this was an *old school* congregation, so anything more would have been too worldly.

DUTCH REFORMED CHURCH OF THE NAVESINK
Marlboro, Monmouth County, 1826

This was known as the "brick church" in an area where brick construction was relatively rare in the early part of the nineteenth century. The church is of traditional Reformed design, somewhat similar to the Reformed churches in Bergen County. Organized in 1699, its congregation is one of the oldest in the state.

(LEFT) FIRST PRESBYTERIAN CHURCH, SHREWSBURY
(RIGHT) OLD SCHOOL BAPTIST CHURCH, HOPEWELL

Hillsborough Dutch Reformed Church at Millstone
Somerset County, 1828

In 1766 the heads of seventy families from six Reformed churches in the area petitioned the elders to establish a new church at Millstone. The first church was probably completed a year later, on land donated by one of the parishioners. That building served until 1828, although it had been severely damaged during the Revolutionary War, particularly after the British sent out a party to capture the preacher, who was, apparently, actively recruiting for the Continental army.

This building is very much in the tradition of the Presbyterian church in Springfield, built forty years earlier, and the Second Presbyterian Church in Elizabeth, built seven years earlier. The symmetrical fenestration and door arrangement are typical of the Georgian style, and can be seen in the Reformed church at Blawenberg and, more modestly, in the Amwell Methodist Episcopal Church built fifteen years later.

DUTCH REFORMED CHURCH OF THE NAVESINK, MARLBORO

HILLSBOROUGH DUTCH REFORMED CHURCH AT MILLSTONE

OLD FIRST CHURCH
Middletown, Monmouth County, 1831

This is probably the oldest Baptist congregation in the state, organized in 1688 by colonists who came from Newport, Rhode Island. The building is a large meetinghouse with a Greek Revival facade.

OLD FIRST CHURCH, MIDDLETOWN

REFORMED CHURCH OF BLAWENBERG
Mercer County, 1832

This large meetinghouse with its Georgian doors was erected in 1832, two years after the church's founding. The quarter-round windows in the gable end are similar to those of the Reformed Church at Millstone, erected two

REFORMED CHURCH OF BLAWENBERG

years earlier, and the cupola that tops the tower is familiar in outline if not identical in detail to those of many contemporary churches.

ALLAIRE VILLAGE CHURCH
Allaire Village State Park, Monmouth County, 1832

This modest-sized Episcopal meetinghouse with its unusual placement of the steeple was built in 1832 for the workers employed at the Howell Ironworks (Monmouth Furnace).

ALLAIRE VILLAGE CHURCH

St. Luke's Church
Hope, Warren County, 1832–1834

This early Gothic Revival church is one of the most distinctive in the state. The belfry is similar to that of several other Episcopal churches built about the same time, but the crenellated battlements are unique. The uniformly cut limestone walls, the quatrefoil recesses, and the delicate tracery in the windows and about the entrance speak of an unusual sophistication in design, which has been attributed to Reverend Peter Jacques. The interior is nearly unchanged, with original box pews and, unusual for an Anglican church, a

St. Luke's Church, Hope

pulpit high above the altar. Hope was settled by Moravians, who left several impressive stone buildings, but only this and a Methodist church remain.

REFORMED DUTCH CHURCH OF CLOVER HILL
Hunterdon/Somerset Counties, 1834

This substantial meetinghouse-style building, erected in 1834, was enlarged by another 15 feet in a totally different style sometime later. The original building had lancet windows, still seen on the sides of the building, while the new front contains round-topped windows and a quatrefoil window set in a rhomboid frame in the tower. The steeple is unique, but the interior is quite traditional, with a gallery around three sides of the building.

CHRIST CHURCH [EPISCOPAL]
Middletown, Monmouth County, 1835

This traditional meetinghouse, with limited Gothic trim, has not been significantly altered since its erection in 1835. It has more in common with the

REFORMED DUTCH CHURCH OF CLOVER HILL

Episcopal church in Shrewsbury, built sixty-six years earlier, than it does with the Episcopal church in Matawan, built fifteen years later under the influence of the ecclesiology movement, which specified Gothic Revival as the only appropriate style for an Anglican church. The builders, William Wood and William Hathaway, completed the work for $1,100 to such acclaim that Bishop Doane proposed to offer it as a model for the smaller churches of the diocese.

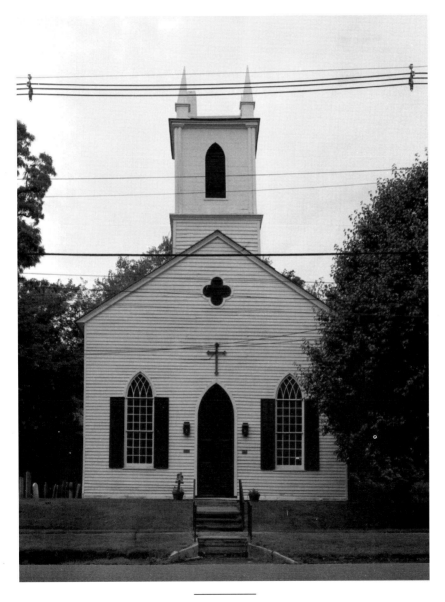

CHRIST CHURCH, MIDDLETOWN

Old Greenwich Presbyterian Church
Warren County, 1835

Founded in 1740, this is the third church and the second stone building on the site. The window-over-door treatment is similar to that of the Reformed church in Neshanic, built more than seventy years earlier.

St. James' Episcopal Church
Piscatawaytown, Middlesex County, 1836

Although it is initially a little jarring, the Greek Revival facade paired with lancet (Gothic) windows is not unusual; Trinity Church in Newark has a similar combination of Greek portico and Gothic windows. There is a small, later addition on the west side of the building, but in other respects, it does not appear to have been modified since its erection. Although the graveyard has been seriously neglected, the church is nicely maintained.

OLD GREENWICH PRESBYTERIAN CHURCH

KINGWOOD PRESBYTERIAN CHURCH
Kingwood Township, Hunterdon County, 1837

Scotch-Irish settlers organized a Presbyterian church in the area by 1736, and a deed to the property in 1745 required the Presbyterian trustees to extend "liberty to the ministers of the Low Dutch Calvinistical persuasion [German

ST. JAMES' EPISCOPAL CHURCH, PISCATAWAYTOWN

Reformed] to preach and perform divine services therein at such times as there is no religious worship performed by the above congregation, freely, peaceably and without interruption." In 1837 the original church was taken down and this stucco-over-stone building erected. It currently serves a Unitarian-Universalist congregation.

KINGWOOD PRESBYTERIAN CHURCH

WITHERSPOON STREET PRESBYTERIAN CHURCH
Princeton, Mercer County, 1837

An early black church in the Greek Revival idiom, this is located a few blocks north of the center of town. The original name was the First Presby-

WITHERSPOON STREET PRESBYTERIAN CHURCH, PRINCETON

terian of Colored, but that was changed to the current name in 1848. The Witherspoon-Jackson section of Princeton was a thriving black community in the nineteenth and early twentieth centuries.

First English Presbyterian Church
Raritan Township, Hunterdon County, 1837

Founded between 1715 and 1733, this modest church, lying a mile from the Old York Road, not only hosted George Whitefield but regularly welcomed an unlicensed Presbyterian preacher, precipitating a schism in the Presbyter-

First English Presbyterian Church, Raritan Township

ian Church between the "old lights" and the "new lights." One group split off to found a new church a few miles away, owing to the fact that there was no tavern in the immediate vicinity where parishioners might restore themselves between the morning and afternoon services.

Musconetcong Valley Presbyterian Church
near Hampton, Hunterdon County, 1838

The mother church for this congregation, Greenwich Presbyterian, lies only a few miles away in Warren County, but members wanting services closer to

Musconetcong Valley Presbyterian Church, near Hampton

home organized the church in 1836 and erected this substantial stucco-over-stone building in 1838. It has been electrified but is otherwise not much altered since; because it is unheated, services are held here only during summer months and on special occasions.

First Presbyterian Church of Cranbury
Middlesex County, 1839

This Greek Revival building was erected in 1839 and extensively remodeled in 1889, although the congregation was careful not to alter the facade. It is wider in proportion to its height than most of the later Greek Revival churches, and the door and window details are different. The steeple is from

First Presbyterian Church of Cranbury

an older tradition and today seems a bit awkward; nevertheless it is an attractive building and a landmark in the area.

FIRST PRESBYTERIAN CHURCH
Basking Ridge, Somerset County, 1839

Although a document in the New Jersey Historical Collection asserts that this church was founded by Scotch Presbyterians about 1700, later scholars assign 1720–1725 as the more likely date. By 1731 there was a log meetinghouse on the site, but when George Whitefield preached to a large gathering in 1740, he spoke in a barn near the church; Whitefield generally drew audiences in the thousands, even in sparsely populated parts of the state. This building has a full Greek Revival portico and a traditional Georgian steeple.

FIRST PRESBYTERIAN CHURCH, BASKING RIDGE

First Presbyterian Church

Princeton, Mercer County, 1839

This church on the edge of Princeton University's campus is the third building on the site, erected in 1839, when the Greek Revival was at the height of its popularity. The architect was Charles Steadman of Princeton, who used this design only three years after it had appeared in New York.

Reformed Church of Griggstown

Montgomery Township, Somerset County, 1843

The church was founded in 1842 and built the following year. By 1851 this Greek Revival plan was duplicated, with minor variations, in more than a dozen other churches, mostly Reformed but including Presbyterian and Methodist, in the immediate area. We know the name of the builder/contractor in several cases, but none of the church records note the architect or source of the plans.

First Presbyterian Church, Princeton

Little York Christian Church
Alexandria Township, Hunterdon County, 1844

Organized at the end of the eighteenth century, the Christian Church was an offshoot of the Puritan Church. This building was erected by a few families who wanted a church closer to home and so split off, with the blessing of the mother church, located a few miles away in Milford. It is an unadorned stucco-over-stone building, now used as a garage/storage barn.

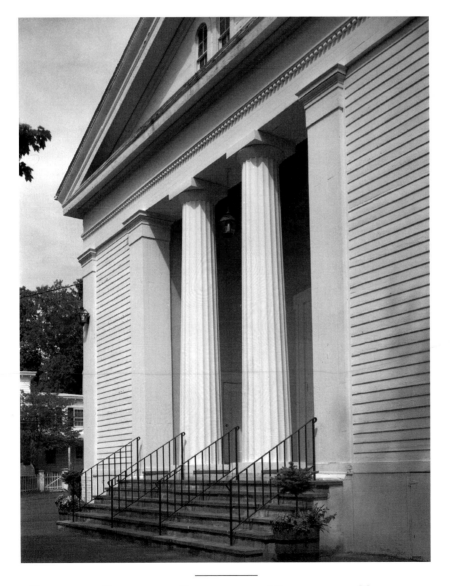

REFORMED CHURCH OF GRIGGSTOWN, MONTGOMERY TOWNSHIP

LITTLE YORK CHRISTIAN CHURCH, ALEXANDRIA TOWNSHIP

SOUTH BOUND BROOK REFORMED CHURCH

South Bound Brook Reformed Church
Somerset County, 1846

Almost identical to the Reformed Church of Griggstown, this was built a couple of years later, a couple of miles away.

Moorite Church, Delaware Township
Hunterdon County, 1849

The German Baptists, also known as Dunkards and today as the Church of the Brethren, settled early in Hunterdon. Their mother church, built late in the eighteenth century, burned in 1950. This church was built by a dissident sect that broke off in 1848 in a dispute that was both doctrinal and personal. The stucco-over-stone building, now being restored, is about as plain as a church can be—no door or window treatment, no steeple, and a single front door.

Moorite Church, Delaware Township

St. Peter's Episcopal Church
Spotswood, Middlesex County, 1849

One of the more important churches in the state from the perspective of the architectural historian, St. Peter's was designed by Richard Upjohn, a leading proponent of the Gothic Revival in this country. The tower is set off to the side of the nave, a common feature of this style, as are the board-and-batten siding and the false buttresses.

St. Peter's Episcopal Church, Spotswood

PLUCKEMIN PRESBYTERIAN CHURCH
Somerset County, 1851

In 1850 the congregation of this church was denied permission to form a Reformed church, so they affiliated with the Presbyterian Church and, a year later, erected this Greek Revival building on the site of a Lutheran church that had been built one hundred years earlier. The congregation also purchased the adjoining lot, on which there was an old Methodist church, tore it down, and built a schoolhouse. This is a very large building; the plan is basically a scaled-up version of the Griggstown Reformed Church.

TRINITY CHURCH [EPISCOPAL]
Matawan, Monmouth County, 1851

Now a restaurant, this building is one of the first examples of a Gothic Revival design for a small rural parish. It has both a transept (crossing) and a chancel, and the steeple is a simple bell cote. Bishop Doane of Burlington, a leading proponent of the English Gothic style for Episcopal churches, laid the cornerstone of this building and was undoubtedly influential in its

(LEFT) PLUCKEMIN PRESBYTERIAN CHURCH
(RIGHT) TRINITY CHURCH, MATAWAN

design. The architect was Richard Upjohn, who more than anyone else popularized the Gothic Revival style in this country. He designed Trinity Church in New York City, but spent considerable time on designs for small, country congregations, often giving away his plans to churches that could not afford to pay an architect.

KINGSTON PRESBYTERIAN CHURCH
Mercer County, 1852

The design of this church comes very close to a traditional New England style. Erected in 1852, it replaced a much older one, built in 1723. The steeple exhibits a mixture of styles, largely Italianate, with its double narrow, arched windows and double brackets.

KINGSTON PRESBYTERIAN CHURCH

St. Peter's Episcopal Church
Perth Amboy, Middlesex County, 1852

Although the town was founded by Scottish dissenters, the first organized religious group was the Church of England. The oldest Episcopal congregation in the state began holding services in the courthouse in 1685 and was officially organized in 1698. Their first church was built in 1721. That was torn down in 1849, despite great opposition because of its history (it had been much abused during the Revolutionary War), and the present building was erected in 1852. Clearly in the Gothic manner, its style is more spare than that of most Episcopal churches of the day, although the interior is very much in the English Gothic tradition.

Presbyterian Church of Lambertville
Hunterdon County, 1855

Although Lambertville was settled a century earlier, the Presbyterians in the area did not organize a church until 1817. This neoclassical building is the third on the site, built in 1855 and enlarged in 1868.

St. Peter's Episcopal Church, Perth Amboy

PRESBYTERIAN CHURCH OF LAMBERTVILLE

REFORMED DUTCH CHURCH OF ROCKY HILL
Somerset County, 1857

In 1856 the building committee of this congregation decided on a plan by H. W. Leard of Princeton, having previously determined that they wanted a Gothic-style building. Leard had designed St. Andrew's Presbyterian Church in Princeton, and probably worked on the refurbishing of Nassau Hall on the university campus. Most of the board-and-batten churches in the state are Episcopal, but otherwise this building is mainstream Reformed-Presbyterian-Methodist in style.

REFORMED DUTCH CHURCH OF ROCKY HILL

Berean Baptist Church
Stockton, Hunterdon County, 1861

Like more than half the churches in Hunterdon, this is a daughter church whose origin is only a few miles away. The rising prosperity of the region after the Civil War prompted a building boom that saw many churches erected by members who wanted to worship closer to home. This building was begun in 1859 and completed two years later. It is built of stone that was plastered in imitation of granite. The original steeple was a multitiered affair, but was replaced by this metal-clad one much later. The building now serves as a Wesley (Methodist) chapel.

Berean Baptist Church, Stockton

Quakertown Friends Meetinghouse
Franklin Township, Hunterdon County, 1862

This area was settled by Quakers very early in the eighteenth century. A deed shows a transfer of land for a meetinghouse in 1733, and there were 240 Quakers living in the county by 1745. Tradition says that some of the stone from the 1747 building was used in the construction of this one in 1862. In 1880 a historian wrote, "[T]he Society [of Friends] is rapidly waning. Only a few of that faith remain in all the region round, but the organization is kept up and meetings are held as regularly as though the house was thronged."[2] This is one of the few stone meetinghouses built by the Quakers and lacks the porches or pent roofs over the doors, but in other respects, down to the iron retainers holding the shutters in place, it is clearly in the Quaker tradition.

Quakertown Friends Meetinghouse, Franklin Township

First Presbyterian Church of Clinton
Hunterdon County, 1864

There is a magnificent exuberance about this building, with its towers, gables, arches, and windows. It was built in 1864, but there were several later additions and renovations. Although it is a very large building (by small-town standards), it does not seem out of scale in the neighborhood, which consists of a number of substantial Victorian residences.

Oldwick Methodist Episcopal Church
Hunterdon County, 1865

Although the area was settled primarily by German Lutherans, Methodists were not long in following. This congregation was founded in 1782 as a Wesley chapel, a dissenting breakaway from the Methodist Episcopal Church. Having outgrown the simple frame building they erected in 1824, they sold it

FIRST PRESBYTERIAN CHURCH OF CLINTON

to a Methodist congregation over the mountain in Califon; it was dismantled and hauled on skids over the snowy road in winter and still sits there by the south branch of the Raritan. The Tuscan arch of the steeple on this building is found in many churches of the period.

St. Peter's Roman Catholic Church
New Brunswick, Middlesex County, 1865

This French Gothic building was inspired by the designs of Richard Upjohn and built in 1865. It sits across the street from Rutgers University, but several blocks away from the center of town when it was built, which is the general pattern for early Catholic churches in this region—even very large ones, such as this. The churchyard wall has been replaced with a wrought-iron gate for privacy and security in this urban setting.

Oldwick Methodist Episcopal Church

ST. PETER'S ROMAN CATHOLIC CHURCH, NEW BRUNSWICK

SIMPSON METHODIST EPISCOPAL CHURCH, PERTH AMBOY

SIMPSON METHODIST EPISCOPAL CHURCH
Perth Amboy, Middlesex County, 1866

This particular design is found throughout the region, but this is the only brick version, and the only one to house a clock in the steeple. The architect was Charles Graham.

FAIRMONT METHODIST EPISCOPAL CHURCH
Tewksbury Township, Hunterdon County, 1868

This is the second church on the site, built in 1868 according to a standard plan used by Methodist, Reformed, and Presbyterian congregations. After repeated lightning strikes, the original 132-foot steeple was replaced by this one about 1900. Wood from the original church, built in 1837, was used to construct a barn a few miles away, which still stands. The reuse of building

FAIRMONT METHODIST EPISCOPAL CHURCH, TEWKSBURY TOWNSHIP

materials is a theme that one finds frequently in church records throughout the eighteenth and nineteenth centuries.

TRINITY CHURCH [EPISCOPAL]
Princeton, Mercer County, 1868

A lovely Greek Revival building was torn down in 1868 in order to build this Gothic Revival structure, designed by R. M. Upjohn, son of Richard Upjohn, who popularized the style in this country. The tower was added a few years later, and major additions were made in 1914–15.

TRINITY CHURCH, PRINCETON

LIBERTY CORNER PRESBYTERIAN CHURCH

Bernards Township, Somerset County, 1869

In the late nineteenth century this hamlet was a retreat and excursion destination. This fine traditional wooden building, with Gothic and Italianate elements, replaced an earlier brick church on the same site in 1869.

LIBERTY CORNER PRESBYTERIAN CHURCH, BERNARDS TOWNSHIP

First Baptist Church
Manasquan, Monmouth County, 1869

The church was founded in 1804 in Ocean County, and this building was erected in 1869. The two towers and shingled facade of the church date to 1898, which is why it looks slightly out of place here. The surface textures of the several varieties of shingles present a marked contrast with the smooth siding on the Liberty Corner Presbyterian Church, built in the previous year.

First Methodist Episcopal Church of New Brunswick
Middlesex County, 1869

By the middle of the nineteenth century we begin to see the name of the architect and not just the builder in church records. In this case, the architect was Augustus Hatfield and the builder, a local architect named Stephen Dettart. The collaboration was a happy one, judging by the results of this unconventional Gothic Revival design.

First Baptist Church, Manasquan

First Methodist Episcopal Church of New Brunswick

St. James' Chapel
Long Branch, Monmouth County, 1869

In serious need of repair, the "Church of the Presidents" has seen seven presidents as worshipers, from Grant to Wilson. The shingle style is the work of Potter and Robertson of New York; the crenellated *keep* to the rear, added in 1893, is probably unique. The building was operated as a museum for a number of years, and now appears abandoned but for the presence of several construction trailers, suggesting that restoration may be imminent.

Bethlehem Presbyterian Church
Union Township, Hunterdon County, 1870

This is an important church in the history of Hunterdon as its congregation was a hotbed of rebellion, sending seven of its members to a meeting of the Sons of Liberty to protest the Stamp Act in 1765. The Presbyterian, Lutheran, and Reformed churches in this part of the state were leaders in the opposition to England; one result was that Hunterdon sent a higher

St. James' Chapel ("Church of the Presidents"), Long Branch

proportion of its population to the Continental army than any other county in the state. In the 1850s the congregation forced out its longtime minister because of his inveterate opposition to slavery, asking for a preacher who "would stick to Christ and Him crucified." This is the fourth church on the site and the second on the same stone foundation. The Tuscan arch is still present in the steeple, but much modified for this Queen Anne version of Gothic Revival.

LOWER VALLEY PRESBYTERIAN CHURCH
Califon, Hunterdon County, 1870

Although the first impression of this building is Gothic Revival, a closer look reveals few of the traditional Gothic elements. It would not seem out of place in New England. In fact, its builders came from a German tradition in the area known as German Valley, a little to the east in Morris County.

BETHLEHEM PRESBYTERIAN CHURCH, UNION TOWNSHIP

LOWER VALLEY PRESBYTERIAN CHURCH, CALIFON

REFORMED CHURCH OF HIGH BRIDGE

Reformed Church of High Bridge
Hunterdon County, 1870

One of the more unusual churches in the state, this Gothic Revival building was designed by George Post of New York, a very well established architect better known for his skyscrapers. He said he was inspired by a Catholic church he saw in France for this design, which contains several traditional Episcopal elements, particularly in the door and window treatment. The original steeple, much taller, was replaced in 1930.

Lebanon Methodist Episcopal Church
Hunterdon County, 1872

Most of the elements of the Gothic Revival style can be found in this substantial church: asymmetrical plan, Gothic arches, false buttresses, variety of window treatments and gables, and several forms of fish-scale shingles. The sheer lack of coherence makes this a fascinating building, as though every member of the congregation insisted on his or her favorite feature, all of which were incorporated. Although Lebanon is a very small town, there is nothing modest about this church, either in scale or in style.

St. Phillip's and St. James' Catholic Church
Phillipsburg, Warren County, 1873

Nineteenth-century Catholic churches are relatively uncommon in the west-central part of the state, as the waves of German Catholic, Irish, and, later, Italian immigrants bypassed the still rural areas for jobs in the cities. Large projects such as a canal or a railroad attracted numerous laborers, who tended to be recent immigrants, so there are pockets of Catholics scattered throughout the region. The gritty town of Phillipsburg on the Delaware had a sufficient Irish and Italian Catholic population by the 1870s to erect this substantial brick Gothic church.

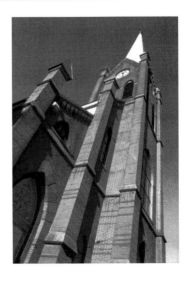

LEBANON METHODIST EPISCOPAL CHURCH

KIRKPATRICK CHAPEL, RUTGERS UNIVERSITY
New Brunswick, Middlesex County, 1873

The triple porch and roof detail mark this building, sited in the oldest part of the Rutgers campus, as of German Gothic design; the architect was H. J. Hardenbergh.

QUAKERTOWN METHODIST EPISCOPAL CHURCH
Hunterdon County, 1878

Two church members drew up the plans and specifications for this building; they stayed within a recognizable style, but added an unusual small vestibule, fish-scale shingles, plus an Empire top to the steeple, which is visible for an extended distance in several directions.

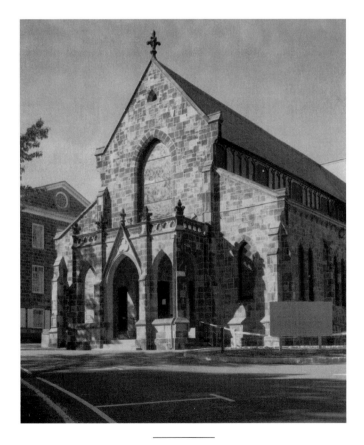

KIRKPATRICK CHAPEL, RUTGERS UNIVERSITY, NEW BRUNSWICK

QUAKERTOWN METHODIST EPISCOPAL CHURCH

St. Paul's African Methodist Episcopal Church
South Bound Brook, Somerset County, c. 1880

It is a nondescript little building that might be mistaken for a small residence in a neighborhood of small residences, but this is one of the few black churches in the area. That is curious because of the substantial black population that lived in Somerset County, dating back to the eighteenth century. More than half the nineteenth-century A.M.E. churches, in fact, are similar—small, one-story vernacular buildings, usually without a steeple. The stained-glass windows are most often the only clue to the religious nature of the buildings.

Presbyterian Church of Flemington
Hunterdon County, 1883

In 1791 a tavern existed where the Civil War monument now stands, and that was the reason why this church is located here. Services in those days were generally morning and afternoon affairs, and the mostly German farm families wanted a place to meet and socialize between sessions. Church records

St. Paul's African Methodist Episcopal Church, South Bound Brook

show the petition for recognition as a separate congregation noted that "no refreshment could be obtained" in the vicinity of their original church. The building is an adaptation of the "Akron Plan," which incorporated the main sanctuary (or a semicircular assembly hall) and two or more tiers of small classrooms opening onto balconies. Akron Plan churches, popular after the Civil War, are usually characterized by a corner entrance and amphitheater seating instead of the long, narrow nave of traditional churches.

First Baptist Church of Freehold
Monmouth County, 1889

Although Baptists settled in the area by the end of the seventeenth century, this congregation was not organized until 1834. The first church was erected in 1848, then greatly enlarged and remodeled in 1869, and replaced in 1889 by this building, designed by Isaac Pursell of Philadelphia. It was originally painted brown with several colors of contrasting trim.

Presbyterian Church of Flemington

First Baptist Church of Freehold

Central Baptist Church
Atlantic Highlands, Monmouth County, 1896

The shingle style is well represented in this fine example of the Renaissance Revival, made popular by architect H. H. Richardson. The oversize "choir" window was typical of Baptist churches of the period.

CENTRAL BAPTIST CHURCH, ATLANTIC HIGHLANDS

BOUND BROOK PRESBYTERIAN CHURCH
Somerset County, 1896

By the end of the nineteenth century, the Gothic Revival had given way to the Renaissance Revival and a host of other variations; this style might be called Tudor Revival from the half-timbered gables and turrets it flaunts. The congregation is one of the oldest in the state, founded early in the eighteenth century.

BOUND BROOK PRESBYTERIAN CHURCH

THORNLEY CHAPEL [METHODIST]
Ocean Grove, Monmouth County, 1897

This small chapel sits only a hundred yards or so from the huge round taber-nacle that has been the center of Methodist revival meetings in Ocean Grove since the 1870s. Its diminutive size is in keeping with the tents and cottages that surround the tabernacle.

THORNLEY CHAPEL, OCEAN GROVE

FIRST BRETHREN CHURCH
Sergeantsville, Hunterdon County, 1898

This church was built by a splinter group from the German Baptist (Dunkard) church a few miles away. The L-shaped design was borrowed from the Methodists, and the fish-scale shingles and other asymmetrical arrangements reflect the high Victorian style. The Brethren are the successors to one of the few Pietist sects that settled in New Jersey; the Ephrata colony, the Amish, and the Mennonites, all in Pennsylvania, come from a somewhat similar tradition, although their approach to church architecture is different.

FIRST BRETHREN CHURCH, SERGEANTSVILLE

NOTES

The Churchscape

1. A. J. Downing, "A Short Chapter on Country Churches," *Horticulturist* 6 (January 1851): 10.

2. Robert P. Bellows, "Country Meeting Houses along the Massachusetts–New Hampshire Line," in *Early American Community Structures,* ed. Lisa C. Mullins (Harrisburg, Pa.: National Historical Society, 1987).

3. Concessions and Agreements, cited in Wallace N. Jamison, *Religion in New Jersey: A Brief History* (Princeton, N.J.: Van Nostrand, 1964), 10.

4. Cited in George L. Smith, *Religion and Trade in New Netherland* (Ithaca, N.Y.: Cornell University Press, 1973).

5. Ibid.

6. Ibid.

7. Cited in Jamison, *Religion in New Jersey,* 11.

8. Bailyn Bernard, *The Peopling of British North America* (New York: Knopf, 1986), 66–67.

9. Ibid., 97.

10. Peter O. Wacker, *Land and People: A Cultural Geography of Preindustrial New Jersey, Origins and Settlement Patterns* (New Brunswick, N.J.: Rutgers University Press, 1975), 132.

11. John R. Stilgoe, *The Common Landscape of America, 1580 to 1845* (New Haven: Yale University Press, 1982), 80.

12. Ibid., 82–83.

13. Ibid., 154.

14. Ibid., 157.

15. St. Peter's Episcopal Church in Freehold had engaged both Robert Smith for the original design in 1771 and Henry Dudley for major renovations in 1878.

16. Henry C. Shinn, *The History of Mount Holly* (Mount Holly, N.J.: Mount Holly Herald, 1998), 39.

17. J. Coleman Hart, *Designs for Parish Churches* (New York: Dana, 1857), and Francis J. Parker, *Church-Building* (Boston: Charles Upham & Co., 1886).

18. Hart, *Designs for Parish Churches,* 7–8.

19. Parker, *Church-Building*, 128–130.

20. Roy Underhill, preface to *Early American Community Structures*, ed. Lisa C. Mullins (Harrisburg, Pa.: National Historical Society, 1987).

21. George Fletcher Bennett, *Early Architecture of Delaware* (New York: Bonanza, 1982), 23.

22. Ellis L. Derry, *Old and Historic Churches of New Jersey*, vol. 2 (Medford, N.J.: Plexus, 1994), 213.

23. Ibid., 171.

24. Parker, *Church-Building*, 25.

25. James Hudnut-Beulmer, *The Many Mansions of God's House*, online at www.material-religion.org/mansions, 1997.

26. Charles D. Cashdollar, *A Spiritual Home: Life in British and American Reformed Congregations, 1830–1915* (University Park, Pa.: Pennsylvania State University Press, 2000), 11.

27. Ibid., 223.

28. Gabrielle M. Lanier and Bernard L. Herman, *Everyday Architecture of the Mid-Atlantic* (Baltimore: Johns Hopkins University Press, 1997), 147.

29. Ibid., 61–62.

THE HUDSON RIVER REGION

1. Ellis L. Derry, *Old and Historic Churches of New Jersey*, vol. 2 (Medford, N.J.: Plexus, 1994), 213.

2. Phoebe Stanton, *The Gothic Revival and American Church Architecture* (Baltimore: Johns Hopkins University Press, 1968), 305.

3. Ibid.

THE DELAWARE RIVER REGION

1. George DeCou, *Burlington, A Provincial Capital*, cited in Ellis L. Derry, *Old and Historic Churches of New Jersey*, vol. 2 (Medford, N.J.: Plexus, 1994), 5.

2. George DeCou, *The Historic Rancocas*, cited in Derry, *Old and Historic Churches*, 58.

3. Thomas Cushing and Charles E. Sheppard, *History of the Counties of Gloucester, Salem, and Cumberland, New Jersey* (Philadelphia: J. P. Lippincott, 1883).

4. Edward Teitelman, "A Queen Anne Quaker Meetinghouse," *Quaker History* 55, no. 2 (1966).

5. Joseph S. Sickler, *The History of Salem County, New Jersey* (Salem, N.J.: Sunbeam Publishing Company, 1937), 87.

6. Stanton, *The Gothic Revival*, 48.

7. Henry C. Shinn, *The History of Mount Holly* (Mount Holly, N.J.: Mount Holly Herald, 1998), 89.

8. Ibid., 55.

9. George R. Prowell, *History of Camden County* (Philadelphia: L. J. Richards & Co., 1886) 129.

The Raritan Valley Region

1. John Lequear, *Traditions of Hunterdon*, ed. D. H. Moreau (Flemington, N.J.: Hunterdon County Democrat, 1957) 127.
2. J. P. Snell, *History of Hunterdon and Somerset Counties, New Jersey* (Philadelphia: Everts & Peck, 1881) 439.

BIBLIOGRAPHY

Amwell First Presbyterian Church of Reaville, N.J. *200th Anniversary, Old Amwell First Presbyterian Church of Reaville, New Jersey.* N.p., 1938.

Andrews, Charles M. *The Colonial Period of American History: The Settlements,* Vol. 3. New Haven: Yale University Press, 1964.

Appleby, Joyce. *Inheriting the Revolution: The First Generation of Americans.* Cambridge, Mass.: Harvard University Press, 2000.

Balmer, Randall. *A Perfect Babel of Confusion: Dutch Religion and the English Culture in the Middle Colonies.* New York: Oxford University Press, 1989.

Bassett, William B. *Historic American Buildings Survey of New Jersey.* Edited by John Poppeliers. Newark: New Jersey Historical Society, 1977.

Beers, F. W. *Atlas of Hunterdon County, New Jersey.* 1873.Reprint, Flemington, N.J.: Hunterdon County Historical Society, 1987.

Bellows, Robert P. "Country Meeting Houses along the Massachusetts–New Hampshire Line." In *Early American Community Structures,* edited by Lisa C. Mullins. Harrisburg, Pa.: National Historical Society, 1987.

Bennett, George Fletcher. *Early Architecture of Delaware.* New York: Bonanza, 1982.

Bice, E. E. *Flemington, New Jersey, Illustrated.* Flemington, N.J., 1898.

Blauvelt, Martha. "Society, Religion, and Revivalism: The Second Great Awakening in New Jersey, 1780–1830." Ph.D. dissertation, Princeton University, 1974.

Bordentown Area Bicentennial Commission. *Bordentown, 1682–1976.* Bordentown, N.J.: Bordentown Historical Society, 1977.

Burchard, John, and Albert Bush-Brown. *The Architecture of America: A Social and Cultural History.* Boston: Little, Brown, 1961.

Butler, Jon. *Becoming America: The Revolution before 1776.* Cambridge, Mass.: Harvard University Press, 2000.

Cashdollar, Charles D. *A Spiritual Home: Life in British and American Reformed Congregations, 1830–1915.* University Park, Pa.: Pennsylvania State University Press, 2000.

Coane, C. B. *The Negro Church in New Jersey.* WPA, 1938.

Converse, Charles S. *History of the United First Presbyterian Church of Amwell, New Jersey.* Trenton, 1881.

Cowing, Cedric B. *The Great Awakening and the American Revolution: Colonial Thought in the Eighteenth Century.* New York: Rand McNally, 1971.

Craven, Wesley Frank. *New Jersey and the English Colonization of North America.* Princeton, N.J.: Van Nostrand, 1964.

Creighton, Linn, and Robert F. Danziger. *The Presbyterian Church in Flemington, New Jersey, 1791–1991.* N.p., n.d.

Cullen, Gordon. *The Concise Townscape.* Princeton, N.J.: Van Nostrand, 1961.

Cushing, Thomas, and Charles E. Sheppard. *History of the Counties of Gloucester, Salem, and Cumberland, New Jersey.* Philadelphia: J. P. Lippincott, 1883.

D'Autrechy, Phyllis B. *Some Records of Old Hunterdon County, 1701–1838.* Trenton, N.J.: Trenton Publishing Co., 1979.

DeCou, George. *Moorestown and Her Neighbors.* 3d ed. Moorestown, N.J.: Historical Society of Moorestown, 1973.

De Lagerberg, Lars. *New Jersey Architecture, Colonial and Federal.* Springfield, Mass.: W. Whittum, 1956.

Derry, Ellis L. *Old and Historic Churches of New Jersey.* Vol. 1. Union City, N.J.: Wise, 1979.
———. *Old and Historic Churches of New Jersey.* Vol. 2. Medford, N.J.: Plexus, 1994.

Dobbins, John K. *Sacred Meaning in Historic Religious Architecture of Southern Illinois.* Online at www.sui.edu, 1997.

Ellis, Franklin. *History of Monmouth County.* 1881. Reprint, Shrewsbury, N.J.: Shrewsbury Historical Society, 1974.

Fabend, Faith Haring. *A Dutch Family in the Middle Colonies, 1660–1800.* New Brunswick, N.J.: Rutgers University Press, 1991.

First 275 Years of Hunterdon County, 1714–1989, The. Flemington, N.J.: Hunterdon County Historical Commission, 1989.

Fischer, David Hackett. *Albion's Seed.* New York: Oxford University Press, 1989.

Garber, John P. *The Valley of the Delaware and Its Place in American History.* Philadelphia: John C. Winston Co., 1934. Reprint, New York: Friedman, 1969.

Gilbreath, S. Burkhart, and Martha H. Gelbach. *Prayers of the Amwell Valley; United First Presbyterian Church of Amwell.* Somerset, N.J., 1987.

Gleim, Elmer Q. *From These Roots–A History of the North Atlantic District, Church of the Brethren.* Lancaster, Pa., 1975.

Gordon, Mark W. "Rediscovering Jewish Infrastructure: Update on United States Nineteenth-Century Synagogues." *American Jewish History* (March 1966).

Greiff, Constance, Mary Gibbons, and Elizabeth Menzies. *Princeton Architecture.* Princeton, N.J.: Princeton University Press, 1967.

Greiff, Constance, ed. *Lost America: From the Atlantic to the Mississippi.* Princeton, N.J.: Pyne Press, 1971.

Gross, Robert A. *The Minutemen and Their World.* New York: Hill and Wang, 1976.

Guter, Robert P., and Janet W. Foster. *Building by the Book: Pattern-Book Architecture in New Jersey*. New Brunswick, N.J.: Rutgers University Press, 1992.

Hagaman, Paul. *One Town Around: A Pictorial History of West Portal and Vicinity*. Asbury Park, N.J., 1984.

Hamlin, Talbot. *Greek Revival Architecture in America*. New York: Dover, 1944.

Hampton, Vernon Boyce, ed. *Newark Conference Centennial History, 1857–1957: A Hundred Years of Methodism*. Newark, N.J.: Historical Society of the Newark Annual Conference of the Methodist Church, 1957.

Hart, J. Coleman. *Designs for Parish Churches*. New York: Dana, 1857.

Herdan, Andrew C., ed. *Rural Recollections: A Narrative and Pictorial History of Union Township*. Union Township, N.J.: Union Township Historical Society, 1988.

History of East Amwell, 1700–1800, A. East Amwell, N.J.: East Amwell Bicentennial Committee, 1976.

History of Three Bridges Reformed Church. 1873. Reprint, Flemington, N.J.: Hunterdon County Democrat, 1973.

Honeyman, A. Van Doren, ed. *Northwestern New Jersey*. 4 vols. New York: Lewis Historical Publishing Co., 1927.

Hunt, Betty Jane. *Wandering West Amwell*. N.p., n.d.

Hunter, Richard W., and Richard L. Porter. *Hopewell: A Historical Geography*. Titusville, N.J.: Township of Hopewell Historic Sites Committee, 1990.

Hunterdon County Planning Board. *Master Plan: Sites of Historical Interest*. Flemington, N.J.: Hunterdon County Planning Board, 1979.

Jacobsen, Douglas. "An Unprov'd Experiment: Religious Pluralism in Colonial New Jersey." Ph.D. dissertation, University of Chicago, 1983.

Jamison, Wallace N. *Religion in New Jersey, a Brief History*. Princeton, N.J.: Van Nostrand, 1964.

Jaquett, Josephine. *The Churches of Salem County, New Jersey*. Salem, N.J.: Salem County Tercentenary Committee, 1964.

Jones, Howard Mumford. *O Strange New World*. New York: Viking, 1964.

Kennedy, Linda Young. *Celebrating a Legacy of Hope: 250 Years of Ministry, 1747–1997, Lebanon Reformed Church*. N.p., 1996.

Kugler, John B. *The History of the First English Presbyterian Church in Amwell*. Somerville, N.J.: Unionist-Gazette Association, 1912.

Lambert, Frank. *Inventing the Great Awakening*. Princeton, N.J.: Princeton University Press, 1999.

Lanier, Gabrielle M., and Bernard L. Herman. *Everyday Architecture of the Mid-Atlantic*. Baltimore: Johns Hopkins University Press, 1997.

Lebanon Township: 200 Years: An Historical Retrospect of Lebanon Township, New Jersey. Lebanon Township Historical Society, 1999.

Leiby, Adrian C. *The Early Dutch and Swedish Settlers of New Jersey*. Princeton, N.J.: Van Nostrand, 1964.

Lequear, J. W. *Traditions of Hunterdon.* Edited by D. H. Moreau. Flemington, N.J.: Hunterdon County Democrat, 1957.

Lidbetter, Hubert. *The Friends Meetinghouse.* 2d ed. York, England: Williams Sessions, 1979.

Listokin, Barbara. *Architectural History of New Brunswick, New Jersey.* New Brunswick, N.J.: Rutgers University Art Gallery, 1976.

Ludwig, Allan I. *Graven Images: New England Stone Carving and Its Symbols, 1650–1815.* Middletown, Conn.: Wesleyan University Press, 1966.

McLaughlin, William. *Revivals, Awakening and Reform.* New York: Harper & Row, 1978.

Mai, Marion. *History of the Amwell First Presbyterian Church, 1738–1988.* N.p., n.d.

Maring, Norman H. *The Baptists in New Jersey.* Valley Forge, Pa.: Judson Press, 1964.

Marrich, John. *In Celebration of 225 Years of Worship and Witness—Zion Evangelical Lutheran Church.* Oldwick, N.J., 1989.

Meeker, Sharon, and Robert Meeker, eds. *The Trial of Rev. Jacob S. Harden.* Legacy of America, 1998.

Menzies, Elizabeth G. C. *Millstone Valley.* New Brunswick, N.J.: Rutgers University Press, 1969.

Morgan, Edmund S. *The Puritan Family: Religion and Domestic Relations in Seventeenth-Century New England.* New York: Harper & Row, 1960.

Mott, George S. *The First Century of Hunterdon County, State of New Jersey.* Flemington, N.J.: Vosseller, 1878.

Myers, Kenneth. *Old Stones at Oak Summit.* Flemington, N.J.: Hunterdon County Democrat, [1983].

———. *Quakertown United Methodist Church.* N.p., n.d.

———. *Scenes of Yesterday.* Flemington, N.J.: Flemington National Bank, 1976.

Naylor, Iris. *Stockton, New Jersey: 300 Years of History.* Stockton, N.J.: Stockton Centennial Committee, 1998.

New Jersey Historical Records Survey Project. *Directory of Churches in New Jersey.* Vol. 10, *Hunterdon County.* Newark: Historical Records Survey, 1940.

Parker, Francis J. *Church-Building.* Boston: Charles Upham & Co., 1886.

Peterson, Charles E., ed. *Building Early America: Contributions toward the History of a Great Industry.* Mendham, N.J.: Astragal Press, 1976.

Podmore, Harry J. *Trenton, Old and New.* N.p.: Kenneth Moore Publishing Co., 1927.

Pomfret, John E. *Colonial New Jersey: A History.* New York: Scribner's, 1973.

———. *The Province of West New Jersey, 1609–1702.* Princeton, N.J.: Princeton University Press, 1956.

Prowell, George R. *History of Camden County.* Philadelphia: L. J. Richards & Co., 1886.

Raritan Township Bicentennial Committee. *Raritan Township, Flemington and Environs, New Jersey.* Flemington, N.J.: [1976].

Rifkind, Carole. *A Field Guide to American Architecture.* New York: New American Library, 1980.

Rose, Harold. *The Colonial Houses of Worship in America.* New York: Hastings House, 1963.

St. Magdalene's Church, 1975. N.p., [1975?].

Savage, Beth L. *African American Historic Places.* New York: Wiley, 1994.

Saxe, Marjorie Ladd. *The Centerville Methodist Church, 1869–1969.* Centerville, N.J.: Centerville Methodist Church, 1970.

Schultz, John H. E. *The History of the Methodist Episcopal Church of Flemington, N.J., 1822–1914.* Flemington, N.J.: Deats, 1915.

Shaw, William H. *History of Essex and Hudson Counties, New Jersey.* 2 vols. Philadelphia: Everts & Peck, 1884.

Shinn, Henry C. *The History of Mount Holly.* Mount Holly, N.J.: Mount Holly Herald, 1998.

Sickler, Joseph S. *The History of Salem County, New Jersey.* Salem, N.J.: Sunbeam Publishing Co., 1937.

Simmons, R. C. *The American Colonies: From Settlement to Independence.* New York: David McKay, 1976.

Sloan, Samuel. *The Model Architect: A Series of Original Designs.* 2 vols. 1852. Reprint, New York: Da Capo, 1975.

Smith, George L. *Religion and Trade in New Netherland.* Ithaca, N.Y.: Cornell University Press, 1973.

Smith, Timothy L. *Revivalism and Social Reform.* New York: Harper & Row, 1965.

Snell, J. P., comp. *History of Hunterdon and Somerset Counties, New Jersey.* Philadelphia: Everts & Peck, 1881.

———. *History of Sussex and Warren Counties, New Jersey.* Philadelphia: Everts & Peck, 1881.

Stanton, Phoebe. *The Gothic Revival and American Church Architecture.* Baltimore: Johns Hopkins University Press, 1968.

Stilgoe, John R. *The Common Landscape of America, 1580 to 1845.* New Haven: Yale University Press, 1982.

Stout, J. E. *Facts and Fantasies of Franklin.* Franklin Township, N.J.: Franklin Township Committee, 1995.

Stroik, Duncan. "Modernist Church Architecture." *Catholic Liturgical Library* (May-June 1997).

Teitelman, Edward. "A Queen Anne Quaker Meetinghouse." *Quaker History* 55, no. 2 (1966).

Thompson, Henry P. *History of the Reformed Church at Readington, New Jersey, 1719–1881.* New York: Board of Publication of the Reformed Church in America, 1882.

Totten, Ada Styles. "Historic Churches in Hunterdon." Manuscript with tipped-in photographs and postcards, 1940. Hunterdon County Library, Flemington, N.J.

Trimmer, William N., ed. *Our Heritage: 125th Anniversary Directory.* High Bridge, N.J.: High Bridge Reformed Church, 1991.

Turner, James. *Without God, Without Creed: The Origins of Unbelief in America.* Baltimore: Johns Hopkins University Press, 1985.

Tyler, Donald H. *Old Lawrenceville: Early Houses and People.* Lawrenceville, N.J., 1965.

Upton, Dell, and John Michael Vlack. *Common Places: Readings in American Vernacular Architecture.* Athens: University of Georgia Press, 1986.

Vecoli, Rudolph J. *The People of New Jersey.* Princeton, N.J.: Van Nostrand, 1965.

Vincent, Lorena Cole. *Readington Reformed Church History, 1719–1969.* Readington, N.J.: The Consistory, 1969.

Wacker, Peter O. *Land and People: A Cultural Geography of Preindustrial New Jersey, Origins and Settlement Patterns.* New Brunswick, N.J.: Rutgers University Press, 1975.

———. *The Musconetcong Valley of New Jersey.* New Brunswick, N.J.: Rutgers University Press, 1968.

Wertenbaker, Thomas Jefferson. *The Founding of American Civilization.* New York: Scribner's, 1938.

Williams, Peter W. *Houses of God: Region, Religion, and Architecture in the United States.* Urbana: University of Illinois Press, 1997.

Wittwer, Norman C. *The Faithful and the Bold: The Story of the First Service of the Zion Evangelical Lutheran Church.* Oldwick, N.J.: Zion Evangelical Lutheran Church, 1984.

Wood, Gordon S. *The Radicalism of the American Revolution.* New York: Knopf, 1992.

Woodward, Major E. M., and John F. Hageman. *History of Burlington and Mercer Counties.* Philadelphia: Everts & Peck, 1883.

Wright, Giles. *Afro-Americans in New Jersey: A Short History.* Trenton: New Jersey Historical Commission, 1988.

Wyckoff, Benjamin. *Historical Discourses Delivered at the 175th Anniversary of the Reformed Church of Readington, October 17, 1894.* N.p., n.d.

Zdepski, Stephen. *The Baptists in Kingwood, New Jersey: A History of the Kingwood Baptist Church at Baptistown and Locktown.* Phillipsburg, N.J., 1974.

INDEX

Adams Methodist Episcopal Church (near
    Swedesboro), 131
Adas Enumo Synagogue (Hoboken), 93
African Methodist Episcopal churches, 72,
    148, 151, 152–153, 223
Akron Plan, 224
Alexandria Township, 169–170, 197–198
Allaire Village Church (Allaire Village
    State Park), 184
Alloway Township, 118
A.M.E. churches. *See* African Methodist
    Episcopal churches
Amwell Methodist Episcopal Church, 21
Anglican churches. *See* Episcopal churches
architects and builders: Eleazar Ball, 56;
    J. C. Cady, 105; James Carpenter, 91,
    104; Stephen Detart, 214; Henry Dud-
    ley, 172; Charles Ellis, 122; Wilson Eyre,
    136; James Gibbs, 25, 28; Charles Gra-
    ham, 211; H. J. Hardenberg, 221; Peter
    Harrison, 25; Augustus Hatfield, 214;
    William Hathaway, 187; Nelson
    Hotchkiss, 30, 138; Inigo Jones, 25;
    Josiah Jones, 25; Charles Keely, 156;
    William Kirk, 68, 74, 77; H. W. Leard,
    205; John Macarthur, 149; Charles
    McKim, 95; John Notman, 41, 69, 142;
    L. J. O'Connor, 87; Jeremiah O'Rourke,
    107; Edward Porter, 86; George Post,

219; Potter and Robertson, 216; Isaac
    Pursell 224; T. A. Roberts, 87; Henry H.
    Richardson, 42, 226; Jacob Reilly, 74;
    Robert Smith, 25, 157, 171–172; Charles
    Steadman, 196; William Strickland, 41,
    136; O. M. Teale, 99; R. M. Upjohn, 212;
    Richard Upjohn, 25, 41, 69, 147, 200,
    202, 209; Samuel Ward, 59; John Welch,
    72; Amos Wilcox, 65; Frank Wills, 41,
    70, 172; William Wood, 187; William
    Halsey Wood, 98; Christopher Wren,
    25, 28
architectural styles: board-and-batten, 200;
    carpenter Gothic, 41–42; English
    Gothic, 33; Greek Revival, 39; Gothic
    Revival, 40–41; Italianate, 42–43; meet-
    inghouse, Georgian, 27, 36–37; meeting-
    house, Quaker, 20, 36–37; neoclassical
    (*see* Wren-Gibbs); Romanesque Revival,
    42–43; schoolhouse, 37–38; vernacular,
    45–46; Wren-Gibbs, 20, 28, 38–89
Arney's Mount Friends Meetinghhouse
    (Springfield Township), 124, 125
Atlantic Highlands, 226
Avas Achim Synagogue (Norma), 160

Baptist churches, 18, 22, 26, 39, 81, 92, 95,
    98, 100–101, 132, 135, 139, 167–168,
    177–178, 179, 182, 206, 214, 224, 226